FINANCIAL INCLUSION FOR MICRO, SMALL, AND MEDIUM ENTERPRISES IN KAZAKHSTAN

JANUARY 2022

ASIAN DEVELOPMENT BANK

ADB

Notes:
In this publication, "$" refers to United States dollars and "T" to tenge.

On the cover: Micro, small, and medium enterprises are the end-beneficiaries of an ADB financial intermediation loan project in Kazakhstan. ADB technical assistance supported regional financial literacy workshops for women entrepreneurs and a forum for light industry enterprises (photos by ADB).

Contents

Tables and Figures

Tables

Figures

Acknowledgments

The author of this report is Sultanova Botagoz, national financial inclusion specialist in Kazakhstan, in collaboration with Catherine Debalucos, project analyst, Elmira Izmaganova, project officer, and Rafael Aquino, associate project officer and under the supervision of Dai Chang Song, principal financial sector specialist.

Special thanks to Tariq Niazi, director of Public Management, Finance, and Trade Division, Central and West Asia Department; and Nariman Mannapbekov, country director of the Kazakhstan Resident Mission of the Asian Development Bank. Appreciation is also expressed for the strong support received from the Knowledge Management Unit of the Regional Cooperation and Operations Coordination Division, Central and West Asia Department.

The peer reviewers for this report were Kelly Hattel, senior finance specialist; Genadiy Rau, economics officer; and Sung Su Kim, finance specialist.

The report was also supported by the Financial Sector Development Partnership Special Fund (FSDPSF) managed by the Sustainable Development and Climate Change Department - Finance Sector Group.

The author also thanks all participants from Kazakhstan, including the microfinance organizations serving the micro, small, and medium enterprises sector, who were involved in the survey as well as in the development and completion of this report.

Abbreviations

ADB	Asian Development Bank
ACC	Agrarian Credit Corporation
Agency	Agency for Regulation and Development of the Financial Market of the Republic of Kazakhstan
AMFOK	Association of Microfinance Organizations of Kazakhstan
COVID-19	coronavirus disease
Damu Fund	Damu Entrepreneurship Development Fund JSC
FCB	First Credit Bureau
IFI	international financing institution
IMF	International Monetary Fund
MFO	microfinance organization
MSMEs	micro, small, and medium enterprises
NBK	National Bank of Kazakhstan
NCE	National Chamber of Entrepreneurs of the Republic of Kazakhstan (Atamaken)
NPL	nonperforming loans
OECD	Organisation for Economic Co-operation and Development
SMEs	small and medium-sized enterprises

Glossary

GPFI	Global Partnership for Financial Inclusion, an inclusive platform for all Group of 20 (G20) countries, interested non-G20 countries, and relevant stakeholders to carry forward work on financial inclusion
household	An economic entity consisting of one or more people living together (it may also consist of a single family or another group of people), combining all or part of their income and property, and jointly consuming goods and services.
individual entrepreneurship	An individual initiative aimed at generating income based on the individual's property and carried out on behalf of individuals, for their risk and under their property responsibility. State registration of individual entrepreneurs is carried out by tax authorities.
Monthly Calculation Index	An index used in Kazakhstan for calculating pensions, allowances, taxes, and other social payments, and for incrementing fines. It is set annually by the law of the Republic on the budget.
operating expense	The sum of personnel and administrative expenses. Personnel expense covers wages and salaries, other short-term employee benefits, post-employment benefit expense, termination benefit expense, share-based payment transactions, other long-term benefits, and other employee benefits. Administrative expense covers non financial expenses (excluding personnel) directly related to the provision of financial services or other services that form an integral part of a microfinance organization's financial services relationship with customers. Examples include depreciation and amortization expenses, rent, utilities, supplies, advertising, transportation, communications, consulting fees, and board fees (European Code of Good Conduct for Microcredit Provision – Version 2.0, June 2013).
peasant or farm household	A family work grouping of persons under which individual entrepreneurship is inseparably associated with the use of agricultural lands designated for the production, processing, and sale of agricultural products.
Portfolio at risk > 30 days ratio (PAR30)	[(outstanding balance portfolio overdue > 30 days / gross loan portfolio) x 100] (Mix Market).
Portfolio-to-assets ratio	(value of gross loan portfolio / total assets) (Mix Market)
Return on average assets	{[(net operating income – taxes) / average total asset] x 100}
Return on average equity	{[(net operating income – taxes) / average total equity] x 100}
Tenge (T)	The currency unit of Kazakhstan

Executive Summary

This report was prepared as part of the Asian Development Bank's Strengthening Micro, Small, and Medium Enterprises Finance Project, which aims to evaluate the access to finance of micro, small, and medium enterprises (MSMEs) in Kazakhstan and identify constraints to and demand for financing.

MSMEs can be a significant driver of economic growth and job creation if they operate in a favorable regulatory environment with good access to finance. The report includes a comprehensive review of the MSME sector as well as the financial intermediaries (banks and microfinance organizations [MFOs]). Considering the significant role of MFOs in broadening the access to financing of entrepreneurs who are not served by banks, attention was given to MFOs using information from interviews with their chief executive officers. The report also brings together the analysis of data from various open sources; however, data derived from different sources are often incomparable, which prevents better analysis and conclusions.

An overview of the key findings and conclusions in the report is presented here.

In 2019, MSMEs contributed about one-third (31.7%) of Kazakhstan's gross domestic product (GDP), growing modestly in the past 3 years (from 25% at the end of 2015) as the sector struggled to recover from the sharp devaluation of the local currency in August 2015. The devaluation severely hit the sector: after a record growth of 34% in 2014, or 1,242,579 registered MSMEs, their number declined by 11% in 2015. By the end of 2019, only 1,330,244 of the 1,603,839 registered MSMEs were active. Nearly half of these (44.3%) were operating in the south of the country and in the capital, specifically in Almaty and Nur-Sultan cities and in the Turkestan and Almaty regions.

MSMEs play a significant role in job creation as they employ 36.2% of the economically active population. Most MSMEs operate in the wholesale and retail trade, agriculture, and services.

Women are relatively well represented in MSME management. In 2019, women-led MSMEs accounted for 42% of all enterprises. The client base of MFOs (as compared to banks) is also dominated by women, with women borrowers accounting for 63.6% of the portfolios of larger MFOs engaged in classical microlending for business.

Recognizing the important role of MSMEs in the economy, the Government of Kazakhstan is making substantial efforts to support them by introducing various financing programs and nonfinancial support services. A number of these programs are operated by the Damu Entrepreneurship Development Fund JSC (Damu Fund) via banks and MFOs. From 2016 to 2019, the Damu Fund financed 45,000 projects with a value of T3.3 billion, of which T1.9 billion was channeled via MFOs (from January 2018 to May 2020).

The agriculture sector is actively financed by the KazAgro National Management Holding JSC, which comprises seven state agencies. The National Chamber of Entrepreneurs of the Republic of Kazakhstan "Atameken" (NCE) and local authorities also provide financial and nonfinancial support for MSMEs.

Second-tier banks remain the main sources of financing for MSMEs and are key conduits of the state's MSME support programs. At the end of 2019, the aggregate small and medium-sized enterprises (SMEs) in the portfolio of the banking sector amounted to $10.4 billion, of which $5.5 billion represented loans to small businesses. The SME loan portfolio of the banking sector has been gradually shrinking since 2016 due to problems in the economy and the banking sector itself.

Compared to the banking sector's portfolio, the MSME portfolio of MFOs is not large, accounting for $770 million in 2019. The aggregate assets of the MFO sector is a mere 1.3% of the banking sector assets, but the loan portfolio of MFOs has increased in recent years, up by 58% in 2017, 37% in 2018, and 34% in 2019. The growth in 2019 was supported by consumption as evidenced by the quicker growth of auto-lending and online platforms. The growth of classical business-oriented MFOs was slower than the market average growth rate. There are now around 200 market players and the sector remains focused on the share of the top 10 companies, which accounts for 83% of overall sector assets. In 2016–2019, new players emerged and quickly grew their market share but these are primarily MFOs engaged in auto- and consumer lending.

In general, the sector has weathered the recent crises quite well, with no high-profile cases of MFOs not being able to meet their obligations. Larger and well-established companies have long-term relations with international creditors as well as established procedures that allow them to keep the overdue loans at a manageable level even during difficult times. At the close of 2019, the aggregate overdue loans of the MFO sector accounted for 7.4% of the total.

The structure of the aggregate MFO portfolio is dominated by loans to individuals for consumer purposes (63% of the total volume at the end of 2019), while 47% of loans are unsecured. The typical profile of the MFO borrower is a microentrepreneur without an established legal entity, who is running a household and a business, where the budgets for both are not separate.

In 2016, MFOs were moved under the regulation of the National Bank of Kazakhstan (NBK), which continues to improve regulatory legislation to strengthen the sustainability of the sector. This includes raising the capital requirement for MFOs and introducing prudential requirement to sub-borrowers and others. These measures are expected to weed out the small and/or inadequately capitalized MFOs with weak procedures. MFOs, which until recently were effectively single-product companies, are also now permitted to offer new services (investment of own assets in securities, factoring, issuance of guarantees, etc.) and to raise funds by placing bonds on the organized stock exchange, with the expectation that larger and more institutionally fit companies will use this as an alternative source of funding. These measures would allow the companies to reduce the cost of funding, which remains high and constraining. The expansion of the range of permitted services of MFOs, coupled with the reduction of the cost of their funding, could enable them to realize their huge potential to address the issue of access to finance.

To assess MSMEs' access to finance, international practice usually takes into account indicators of access to finance and the usefulness and quality of these indicators.

According to calculations made by the authors of the study and based on statistical data, there are 3.3 bank branches (20.8 if all offices are included) per 100,000 people in Kazakhstan, which indicates that the country is behind others in the region when it comes to access to finance. By comparison, this indicator ranges from 26.26 to 36.44 in Uzbekistan, Poland, and the Russian Federation as of 2018.

However, if the regional network of MFOs and KazPost (which acts as the financial services agent) are included as indicators of access to finance, then the absence of physical offices of financial intermediaries can hardly be considered an impediment to access their services.

A larger share of mobile phone users combined with increased internet penetration accelerates the development of digital financial services. In 2018, the population of internet users in Kazakhstan was 81.5%, up from 51.3% in 2011, suggesting that access to the internet has improved, except in rural areas where only 33.6% of the population have access to a broadband connection. The number of mobile phone users is high, with 93% of the population using mobile phones at the end of 2018 (this holds true in the regional, gender, and rural and urban breakdowns).

In Kazakhstan, 17.2% of enterprises (including 12% of small and 27.6% of medium-sized ones) have an outstanding loan or a credit line, while in comparable economies of Europe and Central Asia, the average indicator is 37.5%. This may imply that there is a gap between the demand for and supply of financing. The number of enterprises with rejected loan applications is also high (22.5%), especially among small businesses (36.6%), whereas in Europe and Central Asia, the average rejection rate is only 9.3%. According to the data provided by the First Credit Bureau (FCB) in Kazakhstan, only 12.1% of MSMEs had outstanding loans in 2019, which suggests that access to finance is more difficult for smaller firms: the smaller the business, the lower the share of entrepreneurs with outstanding loans.

Because they consider the operational efficiency of enterprises, banks are more focused on serving medium-sized businesses and larger small enterprises from the small business segment (which among MSMEs have the largest contribution to GDP). When applying for a loan, entrepreneurs have to comply with the strict requirements of banks for collateral, financial reporting, and creditworthiness. The smaller the business, the less prepared it is to meet such requirements as it is less formalized and capitalized, has poorer financial accounting discipline, and possesses assets/collateral in remote regions with low market values. Because of this, MSMEs often opt for quicker loans from MFOs or consumer loans from banks which, although more expensive, do not require collateral and confirmation of business profitability as they are processed through scoring systems. This is confirmed by the growth of the banks' retail loan portfolios and MFOs' portfolios, and aligns with FCB's findings.

According to a 2019 survey by the World Bank, small enterprises in Kazakhstan perceive the practices of the informal sector (19.6%), lack of skilled labor (16.8%), and tax rates (16.5%) as the most significant barriers to finance.

The MSME Finance Gap Report[1] assessed that the financing gap[2] of the formal sector in Kazakhstan is $42.3 billion, while the demand of the informal sector[3] is $35.3 billion. According to the study, only 25% of the formal demand is met. The demand in the current economic environment is undoubtedly less and depends on many factors. Benchmarking on countries with similar economies, nevertheless, showed that the amount of lending to MSMEs in Kazakhstan is lower, and according to the authors' calculations, the MSME loan portfolio in Kazakhstan could be doubled.

The regional distribution of the banks' loan portfolio shows concentration in Almaty and Nur-Sultan cities and in the Karaganda region. There are no statistics[4] on the regional distribution of the MFO loan portfolio (it is very small compared to the banking portfolio). At the same time, the contribution of regional MSMEs to the country's GDP is quite even (Appendix 2, Table 2.2) suggesting that they have a higher demand for financing.

The MFOs in Kazakhstan, engaged in classical lending, have great potential in servicing micro and small enterprises, including the informal sector and rural regions. But the sector needs more affordable sources of funding, technologies to develop relevant digital services, and personnel development. By attracting more players, it is possible to decrease the sector's concentration while increasing its size. This can be facilitated by the development of legislation and regulation; the creation of attractive conditions for investors to the sector; increased market transparency; and higher standards of performance, including the need to collect more detailed statistical information. The maturity, professionalism, and sustainable development of participants in the microfinance sector will lead to their greater contribution to financial services for MSMEs.

---

[1]   According to the MSME Finance Gap Report by the World Bank, International Finance Corporation (IFC), and SME Finance Forum, the demand was evaluated as what it would have been if the enterprises had economic conditions comparable to those in developed economies (methodology described in the report). The MSME finance gap is the difference between current supply and potential demand which can be addressed by financial institutions. The MSME finance gap assumes that the firms in a developing country have the same willingness and ability to borrow as their counterparts in well-developed credit markets and operate in comparable institutional environments, and that financial institutions lend at similar intensities as their benchmarked counterparts.

[2]   Bringing together the potential demand with the current supply produces the MSME finance gap for each country: MSME finance gap = potential demand – existing supply.

[3]   Based on the research of Schneider, Buehn and Montenegro (2010), the employment structure and other macroeconomic factors, such as taxation, regulatory burden, social security, and income level influence the shadow economy or the informal sector. Shneider (2012: 6) defines the "shadow economy" as part of the economy that "includes all market-based legal production of goods and services that are deliberately concealed from public authorities for a variety of reasons." https://documents1.worldbank.org/curated/en/311991468037132740/pdf/WPS5356.pdf.

[4]   Not publicly available.

1 Overview of the Micro, Small, and Medium Enterprises Sector

Role in Economic and Social Development

Kazakhstan remains dependent on oil prices, yet the increasing macroeconomic stability in recent years (2016–2019) and decreasing cyclicality have allowed its economy to respond more effectively to external shocks.[1]

The economy continued to grow as evidenced by the GDP growth rate of 4.1%–4.5% from 2017 to 2019, in line with the long-term government targets, outpacing the global economy in terms of growth rates. Growth was mainly driven by government and quasi-government spending.

Table 1: Main Economic Indicators, 2015–2019

Key Indicators	2015	2016	2017	2018	2019
Nominal GDP (T billion)	40,884.1	46,971.2	54,378.9	61,819.5	68,639.5
Nominal GDP ($ billion)	184.4	137.3	166.8	179.3	179.3
Real GDP growth (%)	1.2	1.1	4.1	4.1	4.5
Nominal GDP per capita ($)	10,509.9	7,714.8	9,247.6	9,812.5	9,686.1
Inflation (%)	13.6	8.5	7.1	5.3	5.4
Average exchange rate (T:$)	221.7	342.16	326.0	344.7	382.7
Agriculture as percentage of GDP (%)	4.8	4.6	4.3	4.3	4.5
Industry as percentage of GDP (%)	24.7	26.1	26.8	28.9	27.2
Services as percentage of GDP (%)	59.4	57.8	57.4	54.4	55.4

GDP = gross domestic product.

Source: Government of Kazakhstan, Ministry of National Economy, Committee on Statistics.

In 2018, the share of agriculture in Kazakhstan's GDP was only 4.3% but the sector remains important as it employs about 13% of all labor resources. Also, 41.5% of the country's population live in the rural areas and these households produce 47% of the gross agriculture output.

The regions with the biggest rural populations are in the south of the country: Turkestan (79.9%) and Almaty (78.0%) (Figure 1). In the Mangistau, Zhambyl, Kyzylorda, North Kazakhstan, and Akmola regions, the rural population is higher than the urban population (excluding the cities of Almaty, Nur-Sultan, and Shymkent).

---

[1] National Bank of Kazakhstan. 2020. *Financial Stability Report of Kazakhstan 2018–1H 2019*. https://nationalbank.kz/file/download/70433.

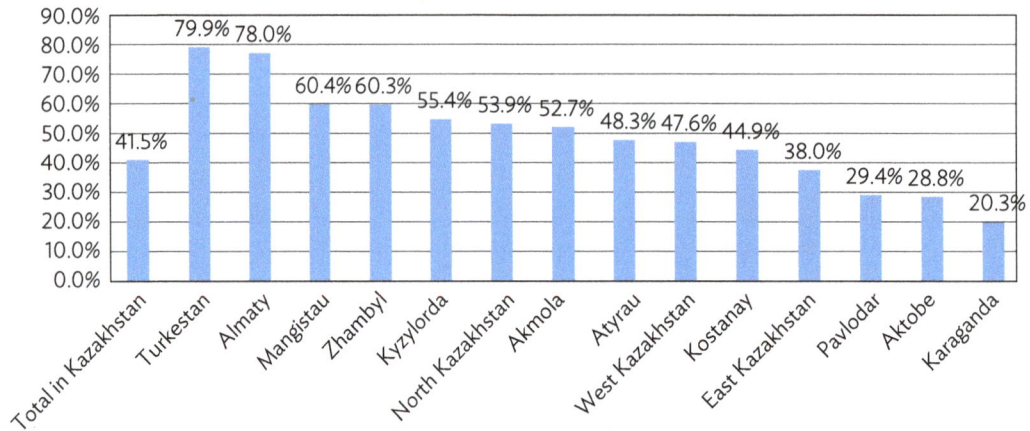

Figure 1: Rural Population by Region

Source: Government of Kazakhstan, Ministry of National Economy, Committee on Statistics.

The population of Kazakhstan continues to grow, accompanied by the growth of its economically active population. The percentage of the population employed by MSMEs in Kazakhstan tends to increase and at the end of 2018, stood at 36.2%. As MSMEs employ more than one-third of the economically active population of Kazakhstan, it plays a significant role in increasing job creation.

Table 2: Labor Force and Employment
(million unless stated otherwise)

Indicators	2010	2011	2012	2013	2014	2015	2016	2017	2018	2019
Total population	16.4	16.7	16.9	17.2	17.4	17.7	17.9	18.2	18.4	18.6
Urban population (% of total population)	54.5	54.7	54.8	54.9	56.5	56.8	57.2	57.4	58.0	58.5
Labor force (over 15 years of age):	8.61	8.77	8.98	9.04	8.96	8.88	8.99	9.02	9.14	9.22
Employees	5.41	5.58	5.81	5.95	6.11	6.29	6.34	6.49	6.61	6.67
Self-employed workers	2.70	2.72	2.69	2.62	2.40	2.14	2.21	2.10	2.08	2.10
Unemployed	0.50	0.47	0.47	0.47	0.45	0.45	0.45	0.44	0.44	0.44
Employed in MSMEs	2.63	2.43	2.38	2.58	2.81	3.18	3.17	3.19	3.31	n/a
Employed in MSMEs (% of total labor force)	30.6	27.7	26.5	28.5	31.4	35.9	35.2	35.4	36.2	n/a

Note: Unemployed refers to registered unemployed people.

Source: Government of Kazakhstan, Ministry of National Economy, Committee on Statistics.

MSMEs are important for the economic and social development of emerging markets. They generate income and create jobs for low-income people. MSMEs drive economic growth, support social stability, and contribute to the development of the private sector. Access to financial services is vital in developing the SME sector in any economy. In emerging economies, MSMEs generate 70%–95% of new employment opportunities. When MSMEs have access to finance, they are more likely to generate jobs, and at a faster rate. However, access to financial services for MSMEs remains severely constrained in many developing countries, restricting business growth. Owners and entrepreneurs report access to capital to be one of their toughest challenges.[2] The succeeding section discusses the key characteristics of Kazakhstani MSMEs and their access to finance.

Main Characteristics of Micro, Small, and Medium Enterprises in Kazakhstan

MSMEs are distinguished by their size, which is measured by the number of employees, the turnover, and/or the balance sheet volume. These indicators, as well as the type of activity, affect the type of taxation regime and the legal status of a business entity.

In Kazakhstan, MSMEs include businesses that meet the following conditions under the Entrepreneurial Code:[3]

- **Microbusinesses**: small businesses with no more than 15 employees and an average annual revenue not exceeding 30,000 Monthly Calculation Index (MCI) (T79.532 million[4]).
- **Small businesses**: individual entrepreneurs and legal entities with no more than 100 employees and an average annual revenue not exceeding 300,000 MCI (T795.3 million).
- **Medium-sized businesses**: individual entrepreneurs and legal entities engaged in entrepreneurship but not related to small and large businesses.

Large businesses include individual entrepreneurs and legal entities with no more than 250 employees but with an average annual revenue exceeding 3 million MCI (T7.953 billion).

For the purpose of state statistics, only the criterion of average annual number of employees is used in Kazakhstan. But for state support and other legislative norm purposes, two indicators are used: the average annual number of employees and the average annual revenue.

In Kazakhstan, the MSMEs' annual gross value added totals T22 trillion, and the MSMEs' share as a percentage of GDP was estimated at 31.7% in 2019. The government wants to increase this to 50% by 2050. The largest contribution to the region's GDP is made by MSMEs in the two largest cities (Nur-Sultan and Almaty), and the smallest one is in the Kyzylorda region (Appendix 2, Table 2.2).

---

[2]   International Finance Corporation. 2017. *MSME Finance Gap: Assessment of the Shortfalls and Opportunities in Financing Micro, Small and Medium Enterprises in the Emerging Markets*. Washington, DC. This study covers 128 countries, of which 112 are low- and middle-income countries. https://www.ifc.org/wps/wcm/connect/03522e90-a13d-4a02-87cd-9ee9a297b311/121264-WP-PUBLIC-MSMEReportFINAL.pdf?MOD=AJPERES&CVID=m5SwAQA.

[3]   The Entrepreneurial Code of the Republic of Kazakhstan. 29 October 2015. No. 375-V ZRK.

[4]   For 2020, the MCI is T2,651.

Table 3: Contribution of Micro, Small, and Medium Enterprises to Gross Domestic Product, 2015–2019

At the End of the Period	2015	2016	2017	2018	2019
Gross value added of MSMEs (T billion)	10,196	12,584	14,257	17,570	22,029
MSMEs as percentage of GDP (%)	24.9	26.8	26.8	28.4	31.7
Including micro and small business as percentage of GDP (%)	20.0	22.1	22.2	22.6	25.5

GDP = gross domestic product, MSMEs = micro, small, and medium enterprises.

Note: The calculations were made taking into account the shadow economy in accordance with the new methodology for assessing the unobserved economy.

Source: Government of Kazakhstan, Ministry of National Economy, Committee on Statistics.

Figure 2: Changes in the Number of Active Micro, Small, and Medium Enterprises, by Year

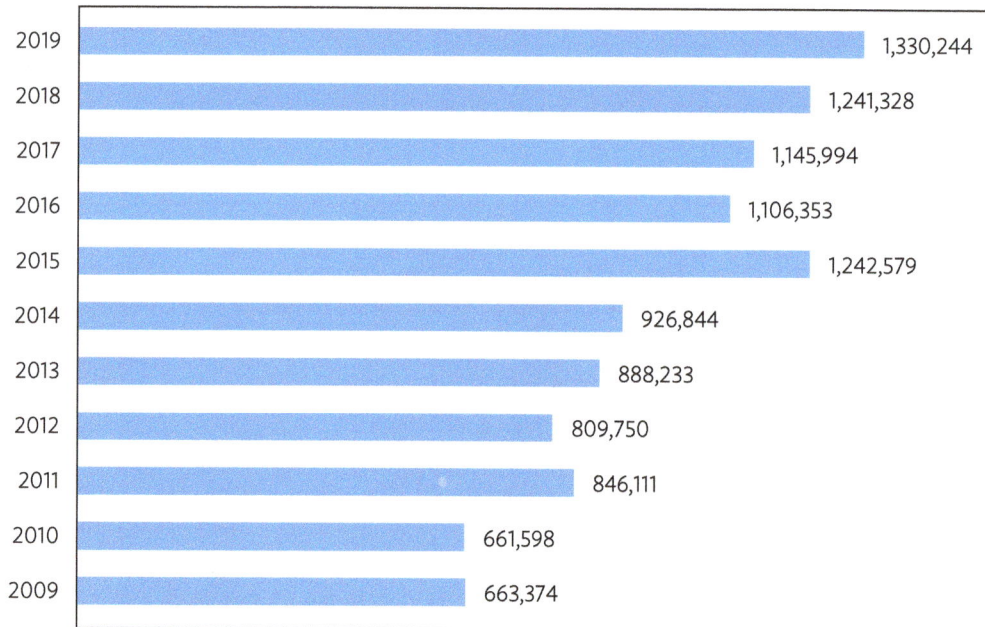

Year	Number
2019	1,330,244
2018	1,241,328
2017	1,145,994
2016	1,106,353
2015	1,242,579
2014	926,844
2013	888,233
2012	809,750
2011	846,111
2010	661,598
2009	663,374

Source: Government of Kazakhstan, Ministry of National Economy, Committee on Statistics.

In 2019, the number of active MSMEs bounced back from the decline in 2016. By the end of 2019, there were 1,603,839 registered MSMEs, 83% of which, or 1,330,244, are active (Figure 2). Of the active MSMEs, more than half (53%) operate in the largest cities (Almaty, Nur-Sultan, Shymkent) and their regions (Figure 3). Majority (64%) are registered as individual entrepreneurs (Figure 4).

Figure 3: Number of Active Micro, Small, and Medium Enterprises in Regions, 2019

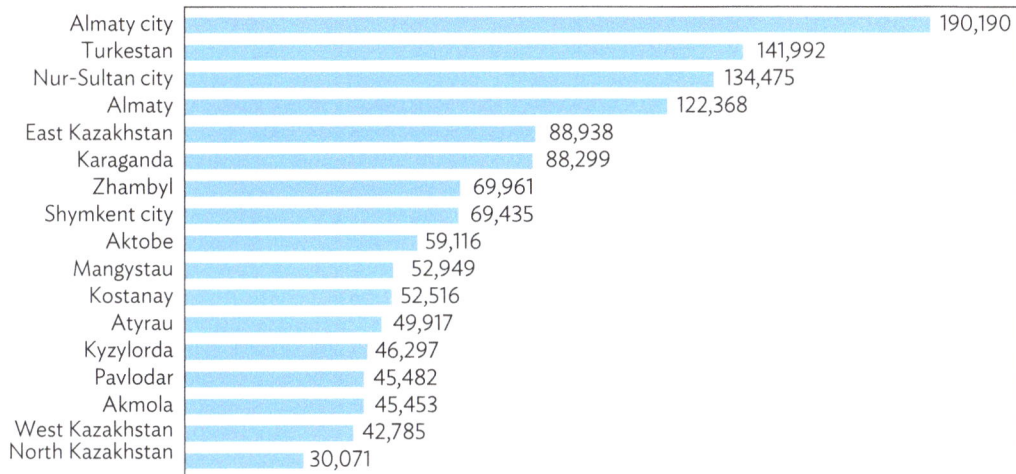

Almaty city	190,190
Turkestan	141,992
Nur-Sultan city	134,475
Almaty	122,368
East Kazakhstan	88,938
Karaganda	88,299
Zhambyl	69,961
Shymkent city	69,435
Aktobe	59,116
Mangystau	52,949
Kostanay	52,516
Atyrau	49,917
Kyzylorda	46,297
Pavlodar	45,482
Akmola	45,453
West Kazakhstan	42,785
North Kazakhstan	30,071

Source: Government of Kazakhstan, Ministry of National Economy, Committee on Statistics.

The largest number of peasant households and farms are registered in the south of the country, specifically in the Turkestan region (71,200) and the Almaty region (45,500). The largest number of the MSME sector's legal entities are in the cities of Almaty and Nur-Sultan (Figure 5). In terms of industry structure, the largest number of MSMEs operate in wholesale and retail trade (33%), followed by the agriculture and services sectors (Figure 6).

Figure 4: Active Micro, Small, and Medium Enterprises by Form of Registration, 2019 (%)

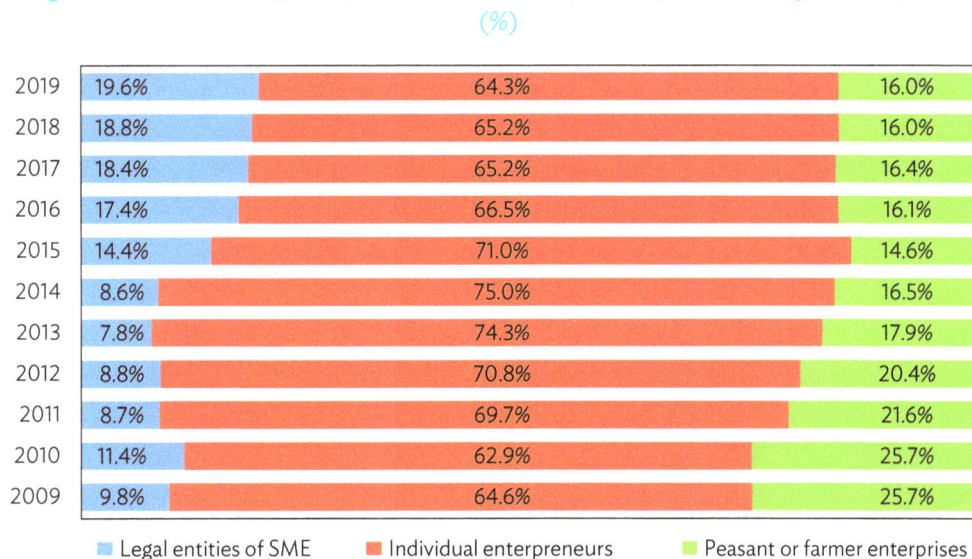

Year	Legal entities of SME	Individual enterpreneurs	Peasant or farmer enterprises
2019	19.6%	64.3%	16.0%
2018	18.8%	65.2%	16.0%
2017	18.4%	65.2%	16.4%
2016	17.4%	66.5%	16.1%
2015	14.4%	71.0%	14.6%
2014	8.6%	75.0%	16.5%
2013	7.8%	74.3%	17.9%
2012	8.8%	70.8%	20.4%
2011	8.7%	69.7%	21.6%
2010	11.4%	62.9%	25.7%
2009	9.8%	64.6%	25.7%

Source: Government of Kazakhstan, Ministry of National Economy, Committee on Statistics.

Figure 5: Active Micro, Small, and Medium Enterprises, by Form of Registration in Regional Split, 2019
('000)

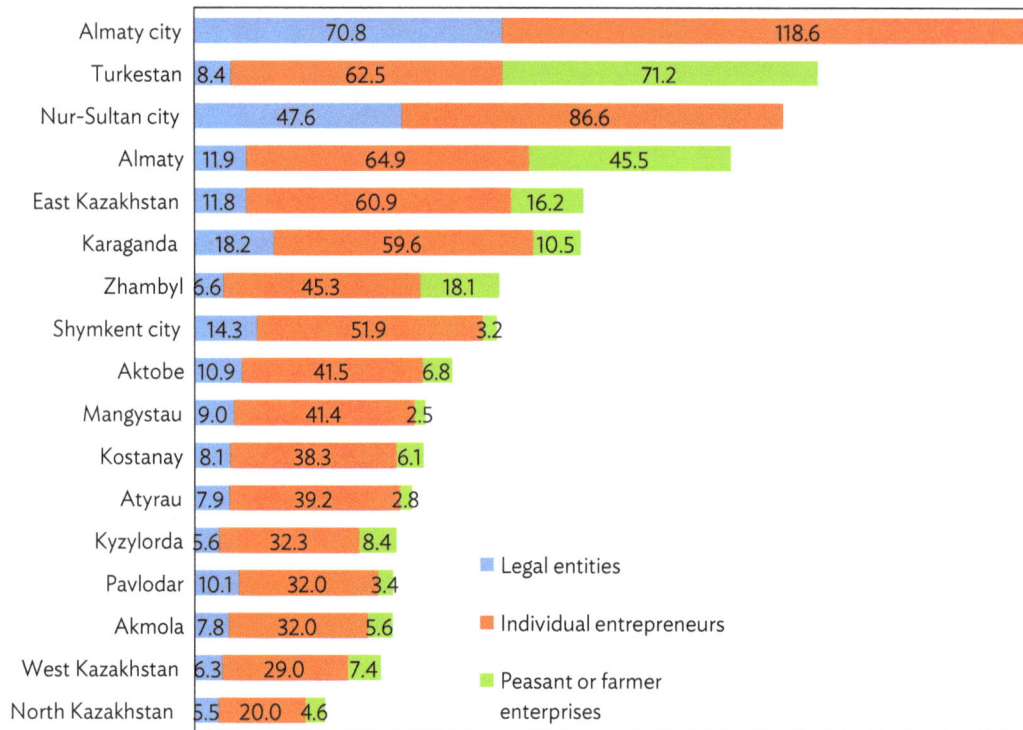

Region	Legal entities	Individual entrepreneurs	Peasant or farmer enterprises
Almaty city	70.8	118.6	
Turkestan	8.4	62.5	71.2
Nur-Sultan city	47.6	86.6	
Almaty	11.9	64.9	45.5
East Kazakhstan	11.8	60.9	16.2
Karaganda	18.2	59.6	10.5
Zhambyl	6.6	45.3	18.1
Shymkent city	14.3	51.9	3.2
Aktobe	10.9	41.5	6.8
Mangystau	9.0	41.4	2.5
Kostanay	8.1	38.3	6.1
Atyrau	7.9	39.2	2.8
Kyzylorda	5.6	32.3	8.4
Pavlodar	10.1	32.0	3.4
Akmola	7.8	32.0	5.6
West Kazakhstan	6.3	29.0	7.4
North Kazakhstan	5.5	20.0	4.6

Source: Government of Kazakhstan, Ministry of National Economy, Committee on Statistics.

Figure 6: Number of Micro, Small, and Medium Enterprises by Industry, 2019
(%)

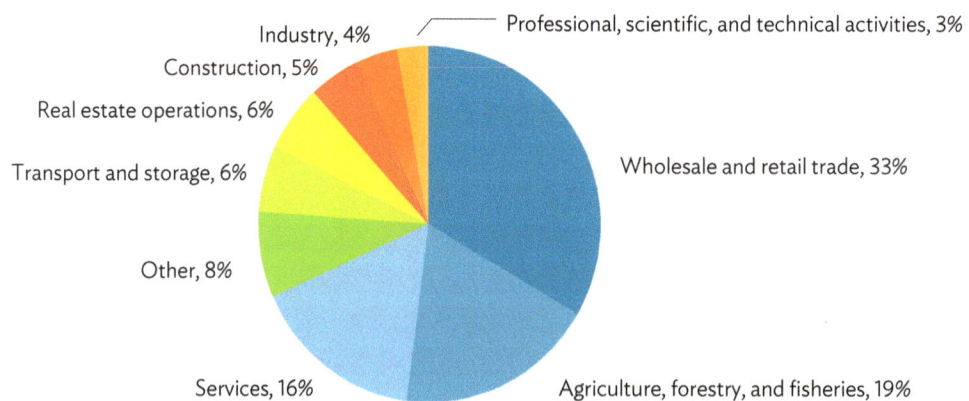

Industry, 4%
Construction, 5%
Real estate operations, 6%
Transport and storage, 6%
Other, 8%
Services, 16%
Professional, scientific, and technical activities, 3%
Wholesale and retail trade, 33%
Agriculture, forestry, and fisheries, 19%

Source: Government of Kazakhstan, Ministry of National Economy, Committee on Statistics.

Figure 7: Micro, Small, and Medium Enterprises' Contribution to Gross Domestic Product by Region, 2019
(%)

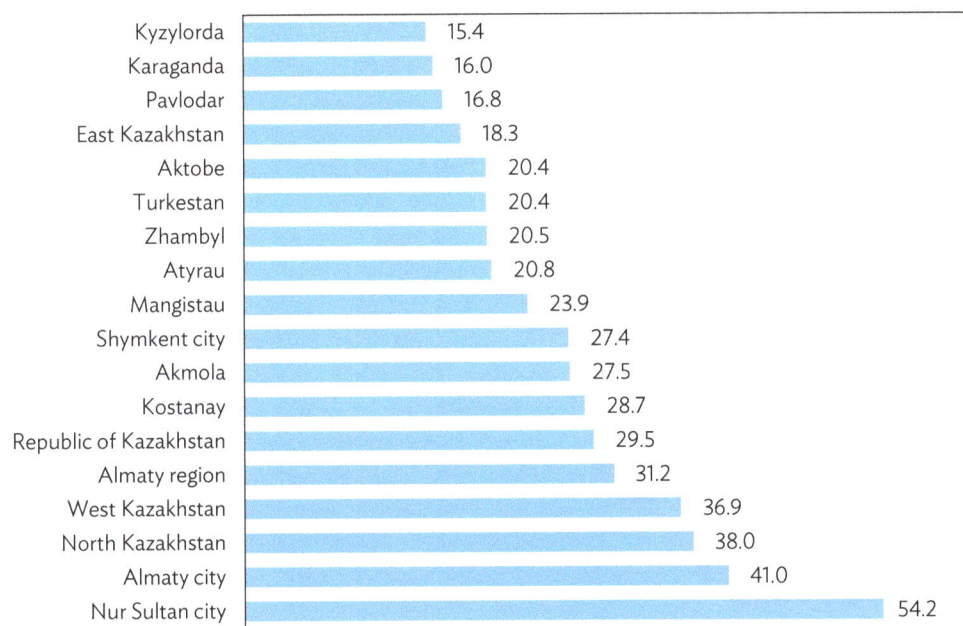

Kyzylorda	15.4
Karaganda	16.0
Pavlodar	16.8
East Kazakhstan	18.3
Aktobe	20.4
Turkestan	20.4
Zhambyl	20.5
Atyrau	20.8
Mangistau	23.9
Shymkent city	27.4
Akmola	27.5
Kostanay	28.7
Republic of Kazakhstan	29.5
Almaty region	31.2
West Kazakhstan	36.9
North Kazakhstan	38.0
Almaty city	41.0
Nur Sultan city	54.2

Source: Government of Kazakhstan, Ministry of National Economy, Committee on Statistics.

Women in Micro, Small, and Medium Enterprises

The share of enterprises headed by women[5] was 42% at the end of 2019. As for the regional split, the smallest number of women-led businesses is observed in the Turkestan region (32%) while the largest number is observed throughout the regions of East Kazakhstan and Karaganda.

However, other studies covering a specific sample of businesses (Table 4) showed only 26% of firms in Kazakhstan had a female top manager. In this study, business owners and top managers in 1,446 firms were surveyed and interviewed in January–October 2019. The international practice uses the percentage of firms with female participation in ownership and with majority female ownership as an indicator of women in business. According to the Enterprise Surveys, women participation in business management in Kazakhstan is higher compared to the Europe and Central Asia region and the developing countries in other regions. However, women's participation in ownership is lower in Kazakhstan than in these countries.

---

[5] The proportion of women in leadership positions is defined as the proportion of women in leadership positions that meet the International Standard Classification of Occupations ISCO-88 in the total employment.

Figure 8: Women-Led Small and Medium-Sized Enterprises, 2019

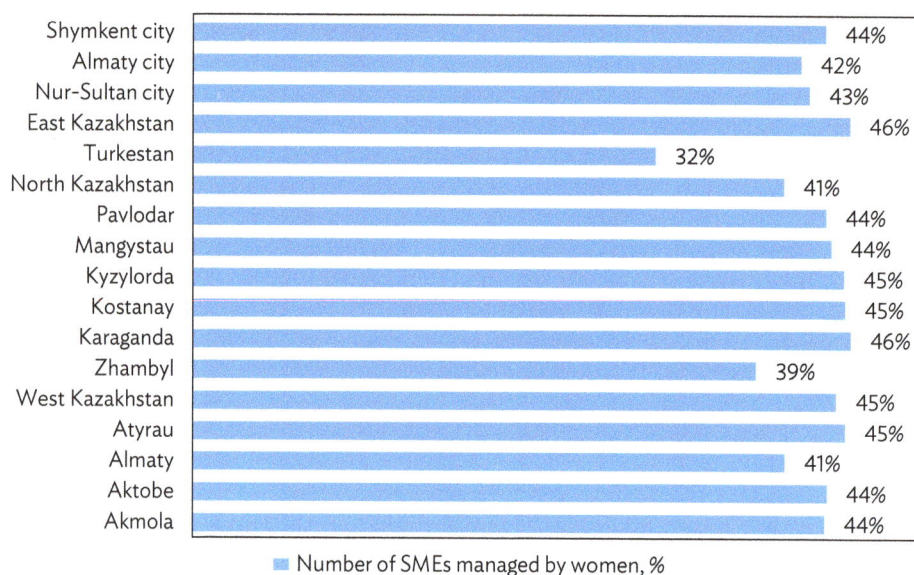

Region	%
Shymkent city	44%
Almaty city	42%
Nur-Sultan city	43%
East Kazakhstan	46%
Turkestan	32%
North Kazakhstan	41%
Pavlodar	44%
Mangystau	44%
Kyzylorda	45%
Kostanay	45%
Karaganda	46%
Zhambyl	39%
West Kazakhstan	45%
Atyrau	45%
Almaty	41%
Aktobe	44%
Akmola	44%

■ Number of SMEs managed by women, %

Source: Government of Kazakhstan, Ministry of National Economy, Committee on Statistics.

Table 4: Women in Business
(%)

Women-Led Firms	Kazakhstan	Europe and Central Asia	128 Countries
Firms with female participation in ownership	30.5	32.4	35.7
Small (5-19)	30.8	31.9	35
Medium (20-99)	29.9	32.1	36.3
Large (100+)	28.6	34.7	37.4
Firms with majority female ownership	23.8	13.8	14.4
Small (5-19)	26.2	15.7	16.2
Medium (20-99)	17.3	10.1	10.7
Large (100+)	12.2	5.8	7.9
Firms with a female top manager	26	18.1	18.1
Small (5-19)	27	19.5	20
Medium (20-99)	25.3	16.1	15.2
Large (100+)	13.4	12.6	12
Proportion of permanent full-time workers that are female	42.6	40.4	33.5

Note: Business owners and top managers in 1,446 firms in 128 countries were surveyed and interviewed in January–October 2019 using the global methodology. www.enterprisesurveys.org.

Source: World Bank. 2019. *Enterprise Surveys* (https://www.enterprisesurveys.org/en/data/exploreeconomies/2019/kazakhstan and https://www.enterprisesurveys.org/en/data/exploreeconomies/2019/kazakhstan#gender).

Access to Finance

To ensure long-term sustainable economic growth, entrepreneurs, regardless of their business size, need access to finance. Financial inclusion means that individuals and businesses have access to useful and affordable financial products and services that meet their needs—transactions, payments, savings, credit, and insurance—and are delivered in a responsible and sustainable way. According to the World Bank Enterprise Surveys 2019, MSMEs are mostly excluded from formal borrowing even if they have an account with a financial service provider.

Table 5 provides an overview of the biggest obstacles to finance experienced by private enterprises in Kazakhstan. The respondents to the World Bank Enterprise Surveys 2019 were asked to choose the biggest obstacle to their business from a list of 15 business environment obstacles. Business owners and top managers in 1,446 firms were interviewed in January–October 2019, excluding these sectors: agriculture, fishing, mining, public utilities, financial intermediation, public administration, education, health, and social work. Also excluded were enterprises with less than five employees, informal firms, and 100% state-owned firms.

The top seven obstacles compared to the regional averages are shown in Table 5.

Table 5: Financial Obstacles for Businesses in Kazakhstan
(%)

Obstacles Cited by Firms	Kazakhstan				Europe and Central Asia	All
	Average	Small (5-19)	Medium (20-99)	Large (100+)	Average	Average
Tax rates	18.3	16.5	26.8	7.1	20.8	12.8
Practices of the informal sector	16.4	19.6	5.9	14.8	13.9	11.8
Inadequately educated workforce	15.8	16.8	12.6	15.2	11.4	7.9
Political instability	8.2	6.7	14.9	1.0	11.3	11.4
Electricity	7.3	8.8	3	3.4	3.7	9.3
Access to finance	7.2	6.6	9.7	4.6	10.5	14.5
Corruption	6.9	8.1	3.3	6.2	5.1	6.9

Note: The number of workers is indicated in parentheses.

Sources: World Bank. 2019. *World Bank Enterprise Surveys.* (https://www.enterprisesurveys.org/en/data/exploreeconomies/2019/kazakhstan and https://www.enterprisesurveys.org/en/data/exploreeconomies/2019/kazakhstan#gender).

The perceptions of managers of large firms are different from the perceptions of managers in medium and small firms. The larger firms have more options in the face of obstacles but they are also more exposed to the failure of the business environment.[6]

According to the 2019 survey, small enterprises consider practices of the informal sector (19.6%), inadequately educated workforce (16.8%), and tax rates (16.5%) as the biggest obstacles to finance. Medium-sized enterprises consider the biggest obstacles to be tax rates (26.8%), political instability (14.9%), and inadequately educated workforce (12.6%).

Only 8.1% of small enterprises and 3.3% of medium-sized enterprises in Kazakhstan that took part in the survey cited access to finance as the biggest obstacle to business development.

The report discusses the indicators of access to financing for MSMEs in Kazakhstan.

The World Bank Enterprise Surveys 2019 used three types of inclusion indicators for the assessment of MSME access to finance: access indicators, usage indicators, and quality indicators. The Global Partnership for Financial Inclusion (GPFI) recommends a wide range of indicators for financial inclusion monitoring. For the purposes of this study, indicators related to business lending were selected from those used in the World Bank Enterprise Surveys.

Access Indicators

Access indicators include the number of bank branches per 100,000 adults and the percentage of adults (aged 15 years old and above) with access to a mobile phone or device, or internet at home. In today's world, with its internet and digital financial services development, clients' physical access to the offices of credit institutions is decreasing as devices or internet-at-home indicators have been increasingly used in recent years.

In 2019, the number of commercial bank branches per 100,000 adults in Kazakhstan increased to 3.3, according to the National Bank of Kazakhstan (NBK). The same indicator calculated for all bank offices, including outlets and points servicing customers, is 20.8 in 2019. The same indicator, including the number of microfinance organization (MFO) head offices is 23.0 (Appendix 2, Table 2.5), showing Kazakhstan to be behind other countries in Europe and Central Asia (Table 6). But the availability of physical offices of financial intermediaries can be hardly considered an impediment to access their services, if the regional network of all bank offices, MFOs and KazPost (which acts as the financial services agent of some banks) are taken into account.

Among the regions of Kazakhstan (Appendix 2, Table 2.5), the largest numbers of banking offices operate in Almaty (336) and Nur-Sultan (182) as of 3 May 2020. There are also significant numbers of bank branches and outlets operating in the Karaganda region (180) and the East Kazakhstan region (177) while there are few banking offices operating in the regions of Kyzylorda (53), Turkestan (55), and North Kazakhstan (59).

---

[6]   This is related to the capacity to navigate business environment obstacles: larger firms may have more options to face obstacles but they are also more visible and more exposed to the failures of the business environment.

Table 6: Number of Commercial Bank Branches per 100,000 Adults

Country	2014	2015	2016	2017	2018
Uzbekistan	43.08	31.06	28.12	38.52	36.44
Russian Federation	34.04	32.93	30.13	29.23	26.26
Kyrgyz Republic	7.89	8.28	8.43	8.18	8.10
Kazakhstan	3.39	2.96	2.95	2.81	2.49
Poland	32.93	31.12	31.01	29.31	29.73
Japan	33.9	34.14	34.10	34.00	34.01

Source: Data from the International Monetary Fund Financial Access Survey.

For the purposes of this study, the number of all bank offices, including branches and outlets, and the number of the registered MFOs were taken into account to calculate the penetration rate in a regional context.

The penetration rate of bank offices and MFO headquarters averages 11.4 offices per 100,000 people across the country and is predictably highest in the cities of Almaty (21.8) and Nur-Sultan (18.0), where the main financial and business activities are concentrated. The lowest branch network penetration rate is in the Turkestan, Almaty, Zhambyl, and Kyzylorda regions due to the high population density in these areas (Figure 9).

Figure 9: Number of Bank Branches and Microfinance Organization Headquarters per 100,000 People

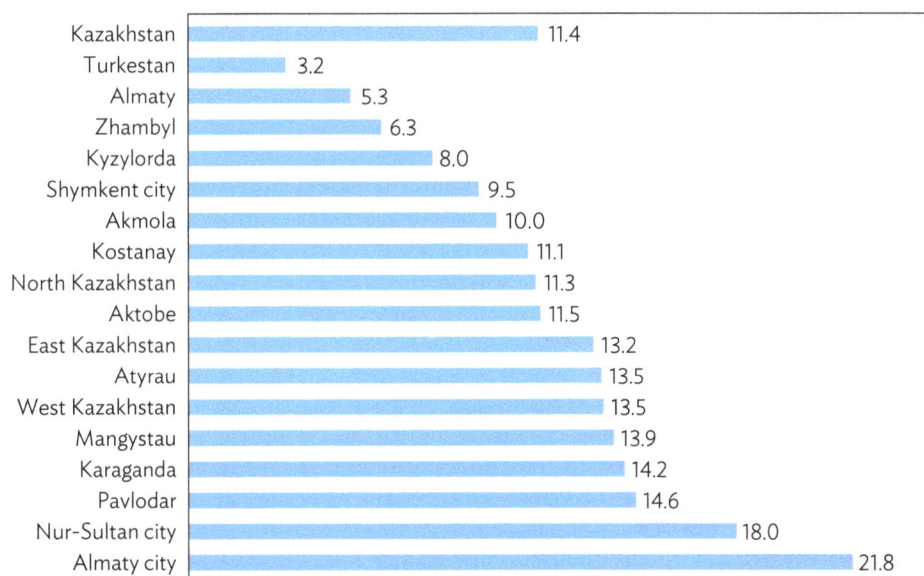

Source: Calculations using data from the National Bank of Kazakhstan and the Government of Kazakhstan, Ministry of National Economy, Committee on Statistics.

Figure 10: Number of Bank Branches and Microfinance Organization Headquarters per 100,000 Active Micro, Small, and Medium Enterprises

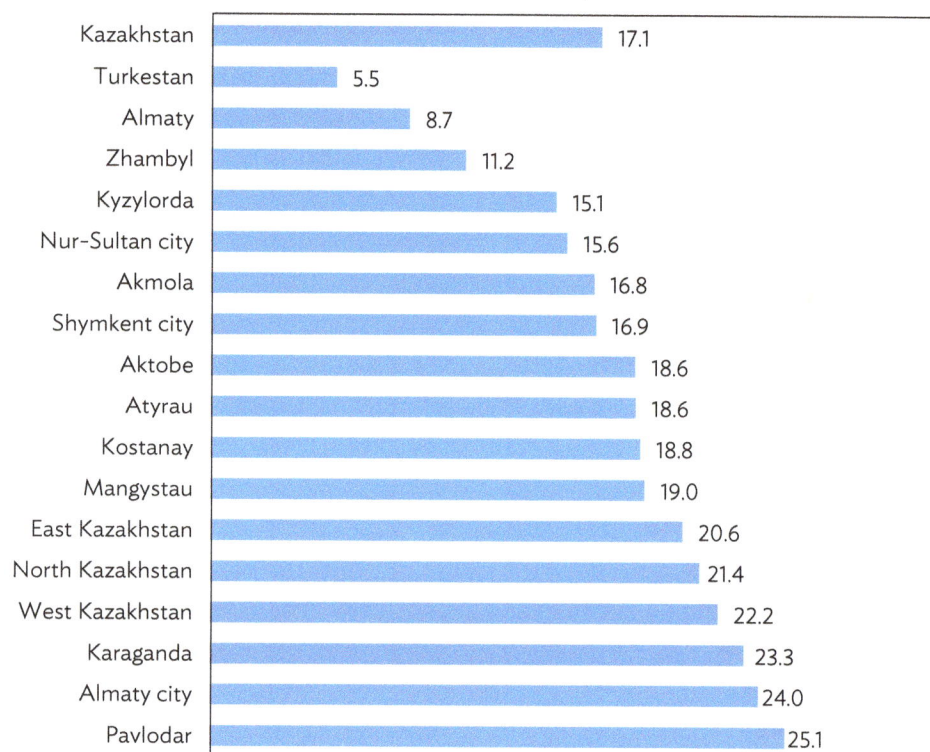

Kazakhstan	17.1
Turkestan	5.5
Almaty	8.7
Zhambyl	11.2
Kyzylorda	15.1
Nur-Sultan city	15.6
Akmola	16.8
Shymkent city	16.9
Aktobe	18.6
Atyrau	18.6
Kostanay	18.8
Mangystau	19.0
East Kazakhstan	20.6
North Kazakhstan	21.4
West Kazakhstan	22.2
Karaganda	23.3
Almaty city	24.0
Pavlodar	25.1

Source: Calculations using data from the National Bank of Kazakhstan.

The situation is similar in terms of the number of bank and MFO offices per 100,000 operating MSME entities: the lowest number of offices serve entrepreneurs in the Turkestan, Almaty, and Zhambyl regions, while the largest number of offices operate in Pavlodar region, Almaty City, and Karaganda region (Figure 10).

Digital technologies play a significant role in bringing people and entrepreneurs access to financial services. To measure access to finance, indicators such as the number of mobile phone users, the proportion of internet users who access the Internet, and the number of internet transactions from and to entrepreneurs' accounts are used.

From 2015 to 2018, the number of mobile phone users in Kazakhstan increased by 10.8%, reaching 93.0% of the country's population by the end of 2018. The high number of mobile phone users is true across regions, gender, and rural–urban divide.

According to the Committee on Statistics of the Ministry of National Economy, the share of internet users using mobile broadband was 81.5% of the population in 2018 (compared to 51.3% in 2011), with internet access remaining low in rural areas, at 33.6%.

Increased mobile phone usage and internet penetration will contribute to the rapid promotion of digital financial services across the country. To speed up economic development and improve people's quality of life through the use of digital technologies, the Digital Kazakhstan State Program has been implemented in the country since 2018.

These prerequisites will fuel the development and growth of digital services in the financial sector of Kazakhstan.

Usage Indicators: Outstanding Loans of Micro, Small, and Medium Enterprises

The usage indicators for MSMEs by GPFI are the percentage of SMEs with outstanding loan or line of credit, the number of SME loan accounts (as percentage of nonfinancial corporation borrowers), and the percentage of SMEs that send or receive digital payments from an account. The analysis of usage indicators in Kazakhstan was limited by data availability.[7]

The Enterprise Surveys in Kazakhstan found that the percentage of SMEs with a bank loan/credit line, i.e., SME loans saturation, is the lowest among the nearest neighboring countries and more than 2.5 times lower than in high-income countries in the Organisation for Economic Co-operation and Development (OECD). On the other hand, the large businesses in Kazakhstan take loans more often compared to those in neighboring countries (60.6%).

Table 7: Usage Indicators

Economy	Year	Subgroup Level	Firms with a Bank Loan or Credit Line (%)	Firms Not Needing a Loan (%)
Europe and Central Asia	2019	Average	37.5	56.7
Kazakhstan	2019	Average	17.2	63.7
		Small (5-19)	12.0	64.2
		Medium (20-99)	27.6	65.9
		Large (100+)	60.6	42.7
Kyrgyz Republic	2019	Average	25.8	69.1
		Small (5-19)	17.4	77.6
		Medium (20-99)	35.3	58.9
		Large (100+)	39.8	57.1
Russian Federation	2019	Average	33.5	42.8
		Small (5-19)	29.9	40.6
		Medium (20-99)	45.4	45.4
		Large (100+)	35.0	66.1

continued on next page

[7]   Many indicator statistics are not gathered at the national level.

Table 7 *continued*

Economy	Year	Subgroup Level	Firms with a Bank Loan or Credit Line (%)	Firms Not Needing a Loan (%)
Tajikistan	2019	Average	18.0	68.1
		Small (5-19)	13.1	69.4
		Medium (20-99)	25.4	65.0
		Large (100+)	32.5	71.2
Uzbekistan	2019	Average	22.2	58.5
		Small (5-19)	18.6	61.0
		Medium (20-99)	29.0	52.3
		Large (100+)	39.3	55.9
High income: OECD economies	**2019**	**Average**	**47.3**	**74.8**
Poland	2019	Average	36.4	71.4
		Small (5-19)	33.9	72.7
		Medium (20-99)	52.5	61.4
		Large (100+)	53.8	71.9
Portugal	2019	Average	47.3	74.8
		Small (5-19)	42.8	80.0
		Medium (20-99)	56.5	65.6
		Large (100+)	74.0	36.4

OECD = Organisation for Economic Co-operation and Development.

Note: For comparison, data on large businesses are also presented.

Source: World Bank. 2019. *Enterprise Surveys.*

The First Credit Bureau (FCB) introduced the Credit Activity Index in Kazakhstan to assess credit penetration, which is the percentage of SMEs with an outstanding loan. The FCB data apply to the entire Kazakhstan market, with several industries included in the World Bank Enterprise Surveys (e.g., agriculture is not involved). The numbers in Tables 7 and 8 are correlated.

Table 8: Credit Activity of Small and Medium-Sized Enterprises

At the End of 2019	Enterprises with Outstanding Loan ('000)	Enterprises with Outstanding Loan (%)
Small and medium-sized enterprises, including:	**150.5**	**12.1**
Medium-sized enterprises	1.1	43.8
Small enterprises	16.0	6.9

Source: First Credit Bureau.

Table 9: Outstanding Loans of Small and Medium-Sized Enterprises from Commercial Banks
(% of gross domestic product)

Economy	2018
People's Republic of China	36.31
Thailand	26.64
Malaysia	20.97
Poland	8.63
Georgia	8.00
United Kingdom	7.83
Kazakhstan	7.38*
Russian Federation	4.06

*In this line, the calculation is based on the data of the National Bank of Kazakhstan and the Committee on Statistics, since there are no official statistics available.

Table 10: Outstanding Loans of Commercial Banks
(% of gross domestic product)

Economy	2014	2015	2016	2017	2018
Japan	95.14	95.46	96.50	98.92	101.17
Poland	47.23	48.22	49.24	47.51	48.18
Russian Federation	46.80	47.29	42.61	41.38	41.70
Uzbekistan	18.15	18.90	21.70	36.55	41.08
Kazakhstan	34.74	33.41	29.21	25.92	23.46
Kyrgyz Republic	19.65	21.82	19.63	20.42	22.95

Source: International Monetary Fund.

The percentage of outstanding loans of commercial banks in Kazakhstan's GDP in 2018 was 23.46%. This includes 7.38% of loans to SMEs, which accounted for 31.45% of banks' total loan portfolio. MSMEs contributed 31.7% (Table 3) to the country's GDP in 2019. Consequently, SME lending by Kazakhstan banks correspond to MSMEs' contribution to the GDP. Approximately half the volume of banks' SME portfolio in Kazakhstan are loans to medium-sized businesses, and although numerous, small enterprises contribute little to the GDP and receive loans in proportion to this contribution.

In addition to the analysis of business lending services indicators, it may be noted that the penetration of bank loans[8] among the economically active population of Kazakhstan is higher than that of corporate business, and has grown over the past few years up to 53% (Table 12). It can be assumed that this is due

---

[8] The penetration rate of loan is calculated as the ratio of the number of borrowers to the economically active population.

to the growth of consumer lending in connection with the introduction of new digital technologies in the market and the simplification of obtaining loans by the population.

At the same time, the household debt to GDP in Kazakhstan is lower (9.7% in 2018) relative to other countries, as well as the total outstanding loans from commercial banks to GDP (see the tables below)

Table 11: Outstanding Loans of Households
(% of gross domestic product)

Economy	2014	2015	2016	2017	2018
Georgia	24.4	27.2	32.1	33.7	36.7
Armenia	22.0	18.2	18.4	18.8	22.2
Kyrgyz Republic	18.1	17.5	16.4	15.5	18.0
Russian Federation	15.1	13.4	13.0	13.6	14.7
Romania	15.2	14.9	14.6	13.9	13.7
Kazakhstan	10.8	11.1	9.4	9.5	9.7

Note: Household debt includes debts with banks and other financial organizations (microfinance organizations, microcredit organizations, etc.).

Sources: National Bank of Kazakhstan *Financial Stability Report 2018–1H2019*; and International Monetary Fund.

Table 12: Bank Loan Penetration among Economically Active Population

Indicator	2015	2016	2017	2018
Number of unique bank borrowers/ economically active population	44%	43%	48%	53%
Average number of bank loans per borrower	1.4	1.4	1.5	1.6

Source: Credit Registry and Government of Kazakhstan, Ministry of National Economy, Committee on Statistics.

Quality Indicators

Quality indicators measure the degree to which the financial products and services match clients' needs, the range of options available to customers, and clients' awareness and understanding of financial products. One such quantitative measure is the percentage of SMEs required to provide collateral on their last bank loan, which reflects the stringent credit conditions.

As seen In the microfinance sector overview, MFOs use a flexible approach to securing loans. For small amounts, a pledge is not required, although the joint liability of third parties is accepted as a form of security. The balance of unsecured loans at the end of 2019 accounted for 77.3% of MFOs' loan portfolios.

The World Bank Enterprise Surveys showed that in providing SMEs loans, Kazakhstan requires moderate collateral coverage compared with regional indicators and has more loans with collateral compared to the Russian Federation and Tajikistan.

Interestingly, Kazakhstan has the highest rejection rate (36.6%) for small firms who applied for loans, especially when compared with other countries in the region: Kyrgyz Republic (7.8), Russian Federation (17.3), Tajikistan (13.7), and Uzbekistan (13.7). The reasons for this could be a lack of transparency in the small firms' financial statements; a large proportion of insolvent enterprises that applied for loans; and a lack of focus of Kazakhstan banks on financing small businesses. More detailed studies would be required to delve into this issue.

According to the World Bank Enterprise Surveys, which covered 1,446 MSMEs, access to finance was more a problem for large and medium-sized businesses than for small ones. However, in Uzbekistan and Tajikistan, fewer small businesses referred to access to finance as a major constraint compared to Kazakhstan.

Table 13: Small and Medium-Sized Enterprises' Barriers to Use of Loans, 2019

Economy	Subgroup Level	Proportion of Loans Requiring Collateral (%)	Value of Collateral Needed for a Loan (% of the loan amount)	Firms Whose Recent Loan Application was Rejected (%)	Firms Identifying Access to Finance as a Major Constraint
Europe and Central Asia	Average	74.3	178.2	9.3	17.3
Kazakhstan	Average	79.3	158.3	22.5	12.3
	Small (5-19)	85.3	153.3	36.6	9.3
	Medium (20-99)	66.2	167.0	6.2	18.5
	Large (100+)	85.9	165.2	2.9	39.3
Kyrgyz Republic	Average	93.6	244.3	7.0	16.7
	Small (5-19)	85.7	273.9	7.8	12
	Medium (20-99)	97.2	227.1	7.9	22.6
	Large (100+)	100	194.1	2.9	21.4
Russian Federation	Average	66.2	176.8	12.7	15.2
	Small (5-19)	59.7	159.9	17.3	11.2
	Medium (20-99)	81.4	192.4	7.3	28.5
	Large (100+)	64.2	147.9	0.6	15.6
Tajikistan	Average	64.2	125.5	9.5	6.1
	Small (5-19)	56.1	98.2	13.7	6.1
	Medium (20-99)	69.1	187.5	6.9	6.9

continued on next page

Table 13 *continued*

Economy	Subgroup Level	Proportion of Loans Requiring Collateral (%)	Value of Collateral Needed for a Loan (% of the loan amount)	Firms Whose Recent Loan Application was Rejected (%)	Firms Identifying Access to Finance as a Major Constraint
	Large (100+)	87.4	n.a.	0	0.9
Uzbekistan	Average	96.4	166.1	15.1	5.8
	Small (5-19)	97.1	172.2	13.8	5.7
	Medium (20-99)	95.1	159.9	17.3	6.2
	Large (100+)	97.5	126.8	10.8	5.2
High income: OECD economies	Average	57.8	88.1	10.9	9.1

OECD = Organisation for Economic Co-operation and Development.

Note: For comparison, data on large businesses are presented.

Source: World Bank Enterprise Surveys 2019.

The availability and list of services offered by financial institutions are analyzed to assess barriers to the use of financial services.

Banks offer their clients a wide range of products and services while MFOs have been allowed limited offerings until recently (Section 4). When interviewed, large MFOs noted that it would be much more convenient for their clients, especially in remote regions, to receive single-window services.[9] But because MFOs cannot offer savings products, cash management services, etc., their clients have to be served by banks and other service providers.

The big challenges for the regions of Kazakhstan are still the clients' lack of awareness of financial products, financial literacy, and the ability to use of digital services (electronic digital signature, banks' mobile services, and digital channels for obtaining and repaying loans).[10]

Assessment of Shortfalls and Opportunities

The challenge of access to finance as a constraint for MSMEs has been thoroughly established through research efforts. MSME data availability and quality in emerging countries remain a significant barrier for research and practitioners. Little research has been conducted about the difference between the supply and demand of financing to MSMEs to determine if a financing gap exists for MSMEs. In recent years, researchers have tried to explore this question for emerging markets.[11] Recognizing the need to

---

[9]   A single window is a system where all facilities are available in one place. For example, in banking there are transactions like withdrawing cash from a savings account, opening a current account, purchasing drafts or pay orders, making fixed deposits, etc.

[10] Based on the current MFOs' survey.

[11] IFC. 2017. *MSME Finance Gap: Assessment of the Shortfalls and Opportunities in Financing Micro, Small and Medium Enterprises in the Emerging Markets.* Washington, DC.

quantify the extent of the MSME finance gap, the International Finance Corporation (IFC) partnered with McKinsey & Company in 2010 to produce an estimate of the gap. The results of the latest study for Kazakhstan in 2018–2019 are presented in Table 14.

The potential demand for MSME finance assumes that the enterprises in a developing country have the same willingness and ability to borrow as their counterparts in well-developed credit markets and operate in comparable institutional environments. In the same way, it assumes that financial institutions have the same willingness and ability to lend as their benchmarked counterparts.

Existing supply/lending to MSMEs by financial institutions was available for 71 countries mainly from the IMF's Financial Access Survey (FAS), and the OECD's SME Scorecard. For the remaining countries, a cross-sectional ordinary least squares (OLS) regression framework was used to predict the missing MSME volume.

Table 14: Number of Enterprises as of 2018

Number of MSMEs ('000)	Micro[a]		SME[b]		Total	
Female[c]	335	30%	34	19%	369	29%
Male	776	70%	145	81%	921	71%
Total	**1,111**	**86%**	**179**	**14%**	**1,290**	**100%**
Financially constrained MSMEs by size[d]	Micro		SME		Total	
Fully Constrained	198	18%	30	17%	228	18%
Partly Constrained	353	32%	36	20%	388	30%
Unconstrained	560	50%	113	63%	674	52%
Total	**1,111**	**100%**	**179**	**100%**	**1,290**	**100%**
Financially constrained MSMEs by sex	Female		Male		Total	
Fully Constrained	71	19%	142	15%	213	17%
Partly Constrained	84	23%	224	24%	308	24%
Unconstrained	215	58%	555	60%	769	60%
Total	**369**	**100%**	**921**	**100%**	**1,290**	**100%**

MSMEs = micro, small, and medium enterprises.

[a] Microenterprises are those with less than 10 employees.

[b] Small and medium-sized enterprises are those with 11-250 employees.

[c] Women-owned enterprises are firms with at least 50% female ownership or female participation in ownership and management (top manager), or sole proprietorships that are female-owned.

[d] Fully credit-constrained firms are those that find it challenging to obtain credit and have no source of external financing. They typically fall into two categories: those that applied for a loan and were rejected; and those that were discouraged from applying either because of unfavorable terms and conditions, or because they did not think the application would be approved. The terms and conditions that discourage firms include complex application procedures, unfavorable interest rates, high collateral requirements, and insufficient loan size and maturity. Partially credit-constrained firms are those that have been somewhat successful in obtaining external financing. They have external financing but were discouraged from applying for a loan from a financial institution, or have applied for a loan that was then partially approved or rejected. Non-credit-constrained firms are those that do not appear to have any difficulties accessing credit or do not need credit. Firms in this category encompass those that did not apply for a loan as they have sufficient capital either on their own or from other sources. It also includes firms that applied for loans that were approved in full.

Source: MSME Finance Gap Report 2019.

Table 15: Financial Access
($ million)

Potential Demand for Finance	Micro		SME		MSME	
Current supply	437	11%	13,831	26%	14,268	25%
Finance gap	3,573	89%	38,740	74%	42,313	75%
Total	**4,010**	**7%**	**52,571**	**93%**	**56,581**	**100%**
Formal Finance Gap	**Micro**		**SME**		**MSME**	
Female	1,208	34%	4,373	11%	5,581	13%
Male	2,365	66%	34,367	89%	36,732	87%
Total	**3,573**	**8%**	**38,740**	**92%**	**42,313**	**100%**
Informal Demand for Finance	**MSMEs**		**Informal Demand for Finance as % of Formal Demand**			
	35,271		**62%**			

MSME = micro, small, and medium enterprise, microenterprise = loans up to $10,000 at origination, SMEs = small and medium-sized enterprises with loans from $10,000 to $1 million at origination.

Source: MSME Finance Gap Report 2019.

Bringing together the calculated potential demand with the current supply produces the MSME finance gap (MSME finance gap = potential demand – existing supply).

The MSME Finance Gap Report assesses the MSME finance gap in countries, assuming what it would have been under favorable economic conditions for operating businesses and with the intensity of supply of financial institutions similar to economically developed countries. The finance gap of Kazakhstan was estimated at $42.3 billion in the formal sector and $35.3 billion in the informal sector. At the same time, the current supply was estimated at $14.3 billion, which meets only 18% of the total demand.

There is no significant gender difference in access to finance in both the microenterprise and SMEs. The share of financially constrained entrepreneurs is 50% in microenterprise and 37% in SMEs. The smaller businesses have less access to finance.

All the MFOs interviewed in the frame of this Asian Development Bank (ADB) study noted an existence of market demand for MSME lending, and pointed out that the growth of MFOs' loan portfolios is related to MFOs' ability to meet customers' needs in products and services.

2　Key Stakeholders in Lending

Damu Entrepreneurship Development Fund JSC

The Damu Entrepreneurship Development Fund JSC (Damu Fund) has over 20 years of experience in supporting SMEs in Kazakhstan.[12] The fund has 17 regional branches operating across Kazakhstan and has significant experience working with local entrepreneurs, public organizations, and local executive authorities.

Baiterek National Managing Holding JSC owns 100% shares in the Damu Fund.

The Damu Fund provides financial and nonfinancial support to SMEs and implements state programs to support them.

Financial support includes:

- facilitating preferential loans through second-tier banks within the programs targeted for regions and individual industries, and microcredit through microcredit organizations;
- subsidizing loans by lowering interest rates on business development loans provided by banks; and
- guaranteeing loans by providing a partial guarantee as a collateral for bank loans.

Nonfinancial support is provided through business service centers:

- free seminars and master classes on specific business directions; and
- free consultation and service support in the most important business areas and state support programs for SMEs.

In 2018, the Apex Department was established in the Damu Fund to provide MFOs access to Yenbek, a productive employment and mass entrepreneurship development program, and Damu-Micro, a program to facilitate quality development in the microfinance sector and build an alternative funding source for micro and small private enterprises.

In 2018–2019, 13 MFOs received T13.6 billion ($33.7 million) in funding from the Damu Fund so they can provide microloans to MSMEs. About 39,000 microbusiness projects were supported through this. The Damu Fund has developed a methodology to evaluate an MFO's performance and then assign a special credit rating to the MFO applying for funding. The funding terms and conditions, particularly requirements for collateral, are determined based on the MFO's rating and credit risk level.

---

[12]　Damu Fund. https://damu.kz/o-fonde/katalog-o-fonde.php.

Banking Sector

In Kazakhstan, banks play a key role in financing MSMEs. One of the key problems of MSMEs is access to funding, primarily associated with limitations such as lack of financial statements, transparency issues, or a weak collateral base. Banks see that there is significant growth potential for lending to SMEs while acknowledging that this direction is tough in terms of the required underwriting functions, technologies, competencies, and skills for credit risk management.

Microfinance Sector

The microfinance institutions play an important qualitative role in providing their customers across the regions with financial services. Unlike banks, they mainly operate in agricultural and remote areas and have lower administrative costs related to regulation. This allows them to remain profitable despite the high operating costs from an extensive network of offices, which is necessary due to the remoteness of the regions and vastness of the country's territories. MFOs are also more flexible with collateral requirements and financial records and statements.

Association of Microfinance Organizations of Kazakhstan

A union of legal entities, the Association of Microfinance Organizations of Kazakhstan (AMFOK) is a nonprofit organization that aims to enhance and promote the interests of its members and the microfinance sector of Kazakhstan.

Established by the country's leading MFOs in February 2004, the AMFOK is the only branch association incorporating organizations interested in the promotion of microfinance in Kazakhstan. It represents the interests of the sector in various forums for financial sector development, takes part in the development of bills for MFOs, and assists members of the association in their activities and issues.

AMFOK has 42 active members whose loan portfolios account for 90% of the total portfolio of the MFO sector. It also has five associate members: First Credit Bureau LLP (FCB), Damu Fund, Smart Pay LLP, Qaryzzaim LLP, and Swiss Capital LLP. AMFOK associate members are organizations that aim to achieve the statutory objectives of the association as well as nonresidents of Kazakhstan.

In 2019, seven MFOs left the AMFOK and nine new members joined the organization. Those that left had difficulties in paying membership dues.[13] In January–February 2020, another two organizations joined the AMFOK.

The AMFOK is accredited in the National Chamber of Entrepreneurs of the Republic of Kazakhstan "Atameken," and is also a member of the Association of Financiers of Kazakhstan, Association of

---

[13]   The Association of Microfinance Organizations of Kazakhstan's annual membership fee depends on the size of the MFO's loan portfolio. It varies from T180,000 for those with a loan portfolio of T50 million to T3 million for those with a loan portfolio of over T20 billion. AMFOK's annual membership fee for associate members is T300,000; for the Damu Fund, the amount is individually determined at T1,270,800. The fees are paid monthly or quarterly in equal installments.

Figure 11: Number of Registered Microfinance Organizations and Association
of Microfinance Organizations of Kazakhstan Members

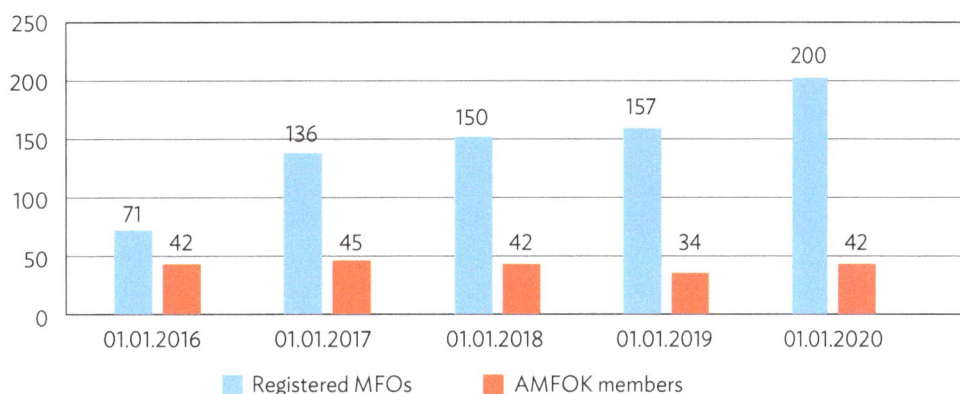

AMFOK = Association of Microfinance Organizations of Kazakhstan, MFO = microfinance organization.

Source: National Bank of Kazakhstan and Association of Microfinance Organizations of Kazakhstan.

Taxpayers of Kazakhstan, and Microfinance Centre for Central and Eastern Europe and Commonwealth of Independent States countries (MFC, Poland).[14]

The AMFOK board of directors includes the heads of large MFOs (Kazakhstan Loan Fund, Toyota Financial Services Kazakhstan, Asian Credit Fund, Arnur Credit, Bereke), the founder of SATOR MFO, and the executive director of FCB.

National Chamber of Entrepreneurs of the Republic of Kazakhstan "Atameken"

The National Chamber of Entrepreneurs of the Republic of Kazakhstan "Atameken" (NCE) represents the interests of small, medium, and large businesses, covering all areas of entrepreneurship including internal and external trade. The primary goal of the NCE is to protect the businesses' rights and interests and to ensure the involvement of entrepreneurs in legislative and regulatory processes affecting business operations.

The NCE has a department for mass entrepreneurship and microfinance to develop mass entrepreneurship projects aimed at increasing business initiatives, mainly in rural regions (e.g., the Bastau Project under the productive employment and mass entrepreneurship development program).

The Fund for Sustainable Development and Support of Women's Entrepreneurship was established in June 2018 as a part of the Fourth Congress of the Council of Business Women of NCE. The fund

---

[14]   The Microfinance Centre is a social finance network that promotes fairness, inclusion, equality, and responsible service. It unites 113 organizations (including 77 microfinance institutions) across 36 countries of Europe, Central Asia, and beyond, who together deliver responsible microfinance services to almost 2 million low-income clients.

implements projects aimed at empowering women who want to implement their business ideas, create new jobs, and raise family income.

International Financial Institutions

International financial institutions also invest in the development of local MSMEs.

Kazakhstan became a member of ADB in 1994. Since then, ADB has committed $5.15 billion in loans and $48.81 million in technical assistance projects, including ADB-administered cofinancing for Kazakhstan.[15] Cumulative loan disbursements to Kazakhstan amount to $4.42 billion. Current ADB operations in Kazakhstan are being implemented under the country partnership strategy for 2017–2021, which is structured around three pillars: economic diversification, inclusive development, and sustainable growth.

To drive investment and generate employment, ADB has been supporting the growth of MSMEs by improving access to finance, particularly for firms located outside major cities and/or operated by women entrepreneurs. ADB provided SMEs specific assistance through loans such as the Small and Medium Enterprise Investment Program – Tranche 3 and the Supporting Resilience of Micro, Small, and Medium-Sized Enterprise Finance Project. A pilot technical assistance and analytical support program is being provided to the government of the Kostanay region to help develop local entrepreneurship. In 2019, ADB also committed an innovative project to give more than 3,000 women access to affordable housing, particularly in rural areas.

In addition to the general financing of the MSMEs of Kazakhstan, the European Bank for Reconstruction and Development (EBRD) implements the Women in Business program and the Regional Small Business Program in Central Asia, offering nonfinancial assistance[16] to MSMEs and financial institutions.

With the support of the Global Environment Facility, the United Nations Development Programme is implementing the Sustainable Cities for Low Carbon Development Project in Kazakhstan to subsidize energy-saving projects totaling about T1 billion.

Various other programs are implemented by international donors and financial institutions.

Quasi-Public Sector

There are two key players supporting agriculture in Kazakhstan.

The first is KazAgro National Management Holding JSC (KazAgro), an organization that brings together seven large state agencies, including the Agrarian Credit Corporation (ACC) and the Fund for Financial Support of Agriculture, which are the major lenders for small and medium agricultural borrowers. The second is KazAgroFinance JSC (KAFI), which operates the state equipment leasing program.

---

[15]   ADB Member Fact Sheet Kazakhstan, updated October 2020.
[16]   Including training, advisory, technical assistance.

KazAgro is involved in state programs to support enterprises in the agriculture sector. In 2018, the share of lending to SMEs accounted for 90.2% of its entire portfolio. KazAgro's consolidated agriculture loan portfolio amounted to T735.3 billion at the end of 2018 (in comparison, second-tier banks' lending portfolio in the agriculture sector was T496.9 billion).

Established in 2001. the ACC is a large financial organization implementing lending programs in priority areas of agricultural production development, defined in the framework of the State Program for the Development of the Agro-Industrial Complex for 2017–2021. The ACC serves over 200 credit partnerships comprising more than 21,000 entrepreneurs across the country. As of 1 February 2020, ACC's loan portfolio was T393.9 billion.

Like the ACC, the Fund for Financial Support of Agriculture lends to SMEs and serves 48,122 active borrowers. In 2019, its loan portfolio grew by 154% to T157.8 billion, as the fund issued 13,500 loans worth T68.5 billion and provided employment for 15,228 people.

Local authorities or regional *akimat* also support SMEs and have helped establish six MFOs in the regions in cooperation with the NCE.

Government Support Measures for Micro, Small, and Medium Enterprises in View of COVID-19 Impact

In response to the coronavirus disease (COVID-19) pandemic, the Government of Kazakhstan declared a state of emergency throughout the country from 15 March–11 May 2020. A number of restrictive quarantine measures were introduced, including restrictions on trade and services and entry into and exit from the country. The government eased quarantine measures beginning 27 May 2020, but increasing morbidity rates in the middle of June caused countrywide strong quarantine restrictions to be declared again on 5 July–16 August 2020.

COVID-19 hit the economy hard, especially the services sector (transport, tourism, catering, cinemas, hotels) and the entire trading sector (excluding the sale of food products and pharmacies). In March and April 2020, the government announced wide-ranging emergency support for MSMEs. Additional funds were approved to implement programs giving preferential loans to SMEs and priority sectors, and those supporting the development of mass entrepreneurship.[17] Financial institutions were instructed to revise repayment schedules for the loans of businesses affected by the pandemic and quarantine measures.

Table 16 presents key government support measures in areas of lending and taxation, which will address the immediate liquidity and credit needs of MSMEs to help them withstand the impact of COVID-19 and protect jobs.

---

[17] State programs to support MSMEs contribute to the strengthening of domestic producers, the preservation of existing jobs, and the creation of new permanent jobs. SME financing in the framework of the state and Damu Fund programs is given on favorable terms—at low interest rates, for long periods. Business loans are subsidized, and guarantees are provided for loans to entrepreneurs with a lack of collateral.

The declaration of a state of emergency and introduction of quarantine measures in the country have had a direct impact on both MFOs and their clients. The Q1 2020 performance results of MFOs showed growth of their portfolio at risk (PAR). In April and May 2020, MFOs provided loan deferrals at the request of their clients and revised debt repayment schedules. According to the large MFOs, up to 60% of their loan portfolios were restructured, and even then, they expect an increase in overdue loan payments due to the impact of the COVID-19 crisis.

Table 16: Support Measures for Micro, Small, and Medium Enterprises Affected
by the COVID-19 Crisis

	Support Measures	Funds Approved/ Terms Provided	Subjects or Conditions
	Lending		
1	Preferential lending program for SMEs	T600 billion ($1.35 billion); second-tier banks' drawdown period is 3 months.	Loans for up to 12 months at a rate not higher than 8% per annum on working capital financing for those affected by the state of emergency and employed within the priority sectors and projects. Limitations for small businesses of up to T3 billion ($7 million) and for entrepreneurs of T50 million ($118,000).
2	Increased funding for the Economy of Simple Things program (and for large businesses)	Up to T1 trillion ($2.25 billion)	6% interest per annum
3	Employment Roadmap	T300 billion ($675 million); additional T84.5 billion ($200 million)	Strengthening measures to support entrepreneurship by subsidizing and guaranteeing entrepreneurs' loans.
4	Enbek program	Additional T50 billion ($118 million)	Developing mass entrepreneurship; establishing an effective model of labor mediation and skills, including support for vulnerable groups
5	Loan obligations deferral, debt repayment schedule reviewing, and other measures.	On a case-by-case basis for up to 90 days	For those whose financial standing worsened as a result of the state of emergency
	Taxation		
6	Property tax for MSME legal entities and individual entrepreneurs	For 2020, the coefficient "0" has been set to the rates	For legal entities and individual entrepreneurs, for taxable items used in tourism, public catering, and hotel services
7	Deadline extension for payment of all taxes and other obligations to the budget and social payments	For 3 months until 1 June 2020	

continued on next page

Table 6 *continued*

	Support Measures	Funds Approved/ Terms Provided	Subjects or Conditions
8	Cancellation of tax imputation and payment and other payments from the payroll budget	For 6 months until 1 October 2020, zero rate applied for taxes and social payments	A list of entities in the most affected sectors of the economy has been approved: in the sectors of trade, transport and technical services, education, medicine, tourism, restaurant and hotel, entertainment, software, and fitness services.
9	VAT deduction (all tax payers)	Until 1 October 2020, VAT rate is at 8%	For sale turnovers and import of staple foods according to the list of socially significant food commodities.
10	Producers of gasoline (excluding aviation) and diesel fuel are exempted from excise tax	Until 31 December 2020	For products sold for export

MSME = micro, small and medium enterprise, SME = small and medium-sized enterprise, VAT = value-added tax.

Source: Overview of Kazakhstani news.

3 The Role of the Banking Sector in Lending

The banking sector is represented by 27 second-tier banks, of which 14 have foreign participation, including 12 subsidiary banks. Since 2014, the number of banks has decreased by 11, but the banking sector concentration continued growing as a result of the reorganization of some banks and the liquidation of others. The top 5 largest banks' share in total assets of the banking sector accounted for 63% at the end of 2019 (compared with 62.4% in 2018).

Table 17: Number of Banks in Kazakhstan

Item	2011	2012	2013	2014	2015	2016	2017	2018	2019
Total number of banks, including:	38	38	38	38	35	33	32	28	27
Banks with 100% state-owned share			1	1	1	1	1	1	1
Banks with foreign capital			17	16	16	15	13	14	14
Bank subsidiaries			14	14	13	11	11	12	12
Share of five largest banks' assets in total banking sector assets (%)	65.3	60	55.4	52.4	59.2	58.2	57.6	62.4	63.0

Source: National Bank of Kazakhstan data reported at year-end.

Due to the sector's reorganization and banks' cleaning up of their nonperforming assets, the banking sector's role in the country's economy has decreased, as demonstrated by its shrinking contribution to the gross domestic product (GDP): from 2016 to 2019, the share of banking sector assets to GDP went down from 58% to 39.6%, and the share of loans from 35% to 22%.

In 2017, the banking sector recorded a loss due to provisions created for a significant part of historical nonperforming loans (NPLs). The following year, it bounced back with a 2.6% return on assets (RoA) and a 21.2% return on equity (RoE). In 2019, the margins further improved to 3.2% and 25.3%, respectively.

NPLs that were that written off also affected the sector's overall dynamics. In 2017, the total assets of banks shrank by 5.5%, followed by a 4.5% and 6.2% growth in 2018 and 2019, respectively. A similar trend was observed for loans and deposits.

In August 2017, the NBK established the Bank Recovery Program, which included the merger of the two largest banks (Halyk Bank and Kazkommertsbank); the NBK's subordination of loans with a maturity of 15 years and low interest rates; the phased injection of new capital by shareholders; and improvements in the regulatory and supervisory frameworks. As part of this program, about T3 trillion of problem loans were bought from the banks' loan portfolio and transferred to the Problem Loan Fund in 2017–2018. This included the historically toxic portfolios of BTA Bank, Bank of Astana, and Tsesna Bank.

Table 18: Financial Intermediation of Banking Sector

Item	2011	2012	2013	2014	2015	2016	2017	2018	2019
Banking sector assets as % of GDP	44.3	45.7	45.1	47.2	57.6	57.6	49.9	42.7	39.6
Loan portfolio as % of GDP	36.0	32.8	38.9	36.7	37.7	35.0	28.1	23.1	21.8
Client deposits as % of GDP	26.9	28.1	28.8	29	37.8	38.9	34.5	29.1	26.6
RoA, sector average %	-0.1	1.9	1.8	1.6	1.1	1.61	-0.25	2.61	3.19
RoE, sector average %	-0.7	28.1	13.2	13.2	9.5	14.94	-2.12	21.24	25.37

GDP = gross domestic product; RoA = return on assets; RoE = return on equity.

Source: National Bank of Kazakhstan.

Table 19: Banks' Assets and Loan Portfolio Dynamics

Indicators	2011	2012	2013	2014	2015	2016	2017	2018	2019
Assets (T billion)	12,817.9	13,880.0	15,461.7	18,239.0	23,784.4	25,566.8	24,157.9	25,244.0	26,809.9
Change in assets (%)		8.3	11.4	18.0	30.4	7.5	-5.5	4.5	6.2
Loan portfolio-principal debt (T billion)	10,472.8	11,657.9	13,348.2	14,184.4	15,553.7	15,510.8	13,590.5	13,762.7	14,742.0
Change in loan portfolio (%)		11.3	14.5	6.3	9.7	-0.3	-12.4	1.3	7.10

bln = billion, KZT = Kazakhstan tenge.

Note: Change in assets pertain to comparison with the previous year.

Source: National Bank of Kazakhstan data reported at year-end.

As part of the NBK's measures to strengthen the sustainability of the local banking sector, external advisors completed in 2019 a comprehensive analysis of the quality of assets of the country's 14 largest banks. This resulted in individual action plans set for several key banks to improve their risk profile and reduce delinquency. These measures are expected to benefit the recovery and improvement of the banking sector's stability.

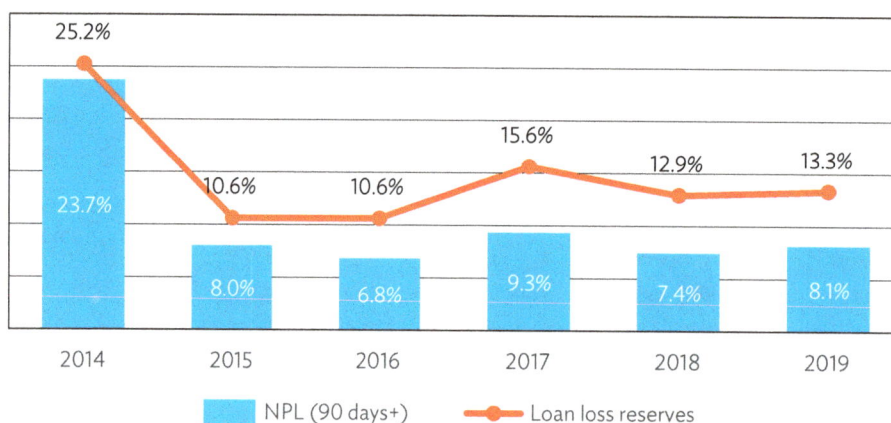

Figure 12: Nonperforming Loans in the Banking Sector

NPL = nonperforming loan.

Note: Nonperforming loans that are overdue by more than 90 days.

Source: National Bank of Kazakhstan.

Banks still serve as the key financial intermediaries providing financing to MSMEs. They are also the major operators of the state support programs for MSMEs, with second-tier banks providing 14.5% of financing under Damu Fund programs in 2018.

At the end of 2019, the share of SME loans in the portfolio of banks dropped to 27% from a high of 34% in 2017. At the same time, the share of individual loans in the portfolio grew from 31% to 43%. According to MFO market participants, one of the reasons behind the retail segment growth is a spillover of loans from the MSME sector to the retail segment, as the procedure for obtaining a consumer loan is faster and easier for a client. The market for credit services is undergoing changes. Banks have begun to build partnership ecosystems with distribution networks and distributors of goods, and to apply digital technologies and scoring systems to quickly process loan applications. These changes primarily affected the retail lending.

Table 20: Loan Portfolio Structure of Banking Sector

Indicators	2013	2014	2015	2016	2017	2018	2019
Total portfolio (T billion)	13,112	13,972	15,422	15,322	13,119	13,489	14,397
Share of corporate loans (%)	56.0	49.5	47.0	42.3	30.9	28.5	27.8
Share of retail loans (%)	24.7	26.1	24.9	24.3	31.3	36.3	42.9
Share of SME loans(%)	17.5	22.9	27.3	32.2	34.3	33.2	26.9

SME = small and medium-sized enterprise.

Source: National Bank of Kazakhstan.

The loan portfolio of credits to SMEs[18] is gradually decreasing, with the volume of loans to SMEs falling to less than T4 trillion in 2019 from a peak value of T5 trillion in 2016. This is despite the large number of preferential financing programs offered on the market. According to the NBK,[19] the role of state financing programs in bank lending is increasing. If in 2014, every 15th corporate loan was issued under the state programs, it was every eighth corporate loan in 2018 (including every fifth recipient of concessional financing).

The portfolio of the banking sector as a whole and the portfolio of loans to small businesses are concentrated in the cities of Almaty and Nur-Sultan. The coverage of lending to regions is insufficient (Table 21).

Table 21: Breakdown of Banks' Loan Portfolio by Region, 2019

Region	Total Loan Portfolio		Small Business Loan Portfolio		
	T million	% of total	T million	%	% of total
Total	13,863,847	100%	203,760	100%	1.47%
Almaty City	7,082,220	51%	122,084	60%	0.88%
Nur-Sultan City	1,708,324	12%	11,233	6%	0.08%
Karaganda	633,518	5%	14,372	7%	0.10%
East Kazakhstan	555,278	4%	8,387	4%	0.06%
Shymkent City	537,352	4%	7,720	4%	0.06%
Atyrau	449,779	3%	3,345	2%	0.02%
Aktobe	382,817	3%	5,083	2%	0.04%
Pavlodar	360,818	3%	5,392	3%	0.04%
Mangistau	357,350	3%	3,608	2%	0.03%
Kostanay	306,443	2%	3,576	2%	0.03%
West Kazakhstan	302,187	2%	3,591	2%	0.03%
Almaty	273,661	2%	1,328	1%	0.01%
Zhambyl	238,869	2%	4,462	2%	0.03%
Kyzylorda	228,541	2%	2,753	1%	0.02%
Akmola	212,281	2%	3,763	2%	0.03%
North Kazakhstan	148,553	1%	2,910	1%	0.02%
Turkestan	85,886	1%	153	0%	0.00%

Source: National Bank of Kazakhstan.

The small business loan portfolio is concentrated in trade, industry, and construction. Statistics show that long-term loans prevail across all sectors, even in trade where the share of long-term loans is 67%.

---

[18] The NBK has not provided statistics on the distribution of SME loans by industry or region, only on small business loans.
[19] NBK. 2020. *Financial Stability Report 2018–1H 2019.* https://nationalbank.kz/file/download/70433.

Table 22: Breakdown of Banking Sector Loans to Small Business by Industry

Industry	Total (T million)	Share of legal entities	Share of individuals	Share of industry	Share of loans in T currency	Share of short-term loans
Trade	544,410	78%	22%	25.8%	81%	33%
Industry	286,264	95%	5%	13.6%	78%	15%
Construction	262,608	98%	2%	12.5%	87%	17%
Transport	120,843	84%	16%	5.7%	83%	16%
Agriculture	97,295	87%	13%	4.6%	82%	17%
Communication	8,518	87%	13%	0.4%	98%	6%
Other industries	788,813	80%	20%	37.4%	79%	4%
Small business portfolio	**2,108,752**	**84%**	**16%**	**100.0%**	**81%**	**16%**
SME loan portfolio	**3,961,800**					
Total banks portfolio	**13,863,847**	**52%**	**48%**		**83%**	**15%**

SME = small and medium-sized enterprises.

Source: Calculations based on data from the National Bank of Kazakhstan.

Table 23: Banks' Loan Portfolios to Small and Medium Enterprises and Microloans of Microfinance Organizations

Year-End 2019	T million	$ million	% of Total Banking Loan Portfolio
Loan portfolio of banks	**13,863,847**	**36,371**	**100.0%**
SME portfolio	3,961,800	10,394	28.6%
Including small business portfolio	2,108,752	5,532	15.2%
Loan portfolio of MFOs	293,336	770	2.1%

MFO = microfinance organization, SME = small and medium-sized enterprise.

Notes:
1. In this table, the currency equivalent is $1.00 = T381.18.
2. The loan portfolio of banks is net of loan loss reserves.

Source: Calculations based on data from the National Bank of Kazakhstan.

Most of the loans to small businesses (81%) were issued in the local currency. Loan recipients were mainly legal entities (84%).

At the end of 2019, the share of SME portfolio accounted for 28.6% of the banking sector's total portfolio; 15.2% of SME portfolio were small businesses. The MFOs' portfolio is tiny and accounts for only 2.1% of the banking sector loan portfolio.

4 Overview of the Microfinance Sector

Introduction

There are several broad groups of MFOs operating in the market:

Classic MFOs. These are companies that were originally set up to fill the financing gap by covering the needs of people perceived as unbankable or who have difficulties accessing finance. These MFOs issue loans in physical offices and online, and target microbusinesses and individuals outside of large cities, which are not covered by banks. These companies have special lending methodologies and other required resources (trained staff, regional presence, information technology, etc.) to assess and take on a more sophisticated risk of longer maturity. Because they apply market-based principles in their operations (e.g., interest rates determination, creditworthiness assessment), they are self-sustainable and able to tap commercial sources of debt and equity funding including international financial institutions. Kazakhstan Loan Fund (KMF), Arnur Credit, and Asian Credit Fund are examples of such companies in the top 10 MFOs.

Quasi-government/municipal MFOs. In 2016, the government initiated a state program of microlending where funding was available at 2% interest rate (with the rate for the final borrower at 6%). A number of regional MFOs were set up by local *akimat* and/or the NCE as conduits for this funding, e.g., Atameken Taraz, Atameken Pavlodar, Atameken Atyrau. Because these MFOs issue subsidized loans below market rates, which do not cover their expenses, they are not self-sustainable. Their viability and operations depend on the continued financial support from the parent/state budget.

Captive MFOs. These are subsidiaries of larger industrial or financial groups which set up their own microfinancing entity to facilitate sales at the group level and/or to comply with the local regulation. As a rule, these are mono-product companies serving the interests of the group (e.g. selling only auto loans) and have little independence or need to source financing and clients. Some captive MFOs that specialize in auto-lending are Toyota Financial Services, Shinhan Finance, and MC-Finance formed by Astana Motors KMC and BNK Finance Kazakhstan.

Online platforms. These are companies that issue quick, unsecured loans online within minutes and require minimum documentation, which makes them more attractive than the classical MFOs with tedious administrative paperwork. These platforms do standard checks with the credit bureau, review social network profiles, and conduct telephone interviews so the loan can be issued without the client having to visit their office. Typically, they have limited or no regional presence as they can lend to anyone anywhere as long as there is internet connectivity. All they require are an ID, electronic signature, and a bank or card account where they can transfer loan proceeds. These quick loans are very convenient to individuals to cover temporary liquidity shortages or unexpected expenses (also called an "until-the-salary loan"). OnlineKazFinance (under the brand name Solva) is one of the larger of such online platforms in the local market, with many other smaller players.

Table 24: Classification of the Top 10 Microfinance Organizations

Rank by Assets	Microfinance Organizations	Classical	Captive	Online	Quasi-State/ State Programs
1	Kazakhstan Loan Fund	x			
2	Toyota Financial Services		x		
3	OnlineKazFinance (Solva)			x	
4	Arnur Credit	x			
5	Yrys				x
6	Asian Credit Fund	x			
7	Shinhan Finance		x		
8	Regional Investment Center (Kyzylorda)				x
9	BNK Finance		x		
10	MC-Finance		x		

Source: Classified by the author of the study based on the collected data.

Regulatory Framework and Prudential Requirements

Since January 2016, the operations of MFOs have been regulated by the NBK. From being covered by the Civil Code, which stipulated requirements for their organization and operations,[20] with no prudential supervision, MFOs were placed under the supervision of the NBK to bring more transparency in their operations and increase their stability. They were required to pass state re-registration and ensure a minimum capital (T30 million). This benefited the sector as it forced weaker MFOs to leave the market while strengthening the financial sector as borrowers of MFOs were now also covered by the First Credit Bureau (FCB).

At the beginning of 2020, there were 199 MFOs registered by the NBK. Their operations are regulated by the Agency for Regulation and Development of the Financial Market (Agency), which was separated from the NBK in 2019.

Below is the historical data on the number of MFOs before and after the registration.

Table 25: Changes in the Number of Microfinance Organizations, 2007–2016

2007	2008	2009	2010	2011	2012	2013	2014	2015	2016	2017	2018	2019
745	1,086	1,317	1,712	1,780	1,756	1,766	1,706	1,643	136	150	157	199

Note: By 2015, there were requirements for minimum capital, maximum interest rate, and maximum loan size.
Sources: Association of Microfinance Organizations of Kazakhstan; Government of Kazakhstan, Ministry of National Economy, Committee on Statistics; and National Bank of Kazakhstan.

---

20   There were requirements for minimum capital, maximum interest rate, and maximum loan size.

The operations of MFOs are covered by the Constitution, the Civil Code, and the law on microfinance activities and other regulatory legal acts. As per the original law,[21] MFOs were limited to issuing microloans with a maximum size of 8,000 Monthly Calculation Index (MCI)[22] and an interest rate capped at 56%. In 2020, MFOs were allowed to expand their operations by investing their own assets in securities, carrying out factoring and forfeiting operations, issuing guarantees, and serving as payment and billing agents.[23] The regulator also permitted MFOs to be established as joint-stock companies (previously only as business partnerships) and to issue and place bonds in the organized securities market. The maximum loan size was raised from 8,000 MCI to 25,000 MCI.[24] The services on opening of accounts, remittances, and foreign exchange operations, which MFOs had been lobbying for and which can make their services more comprehensive, were not included in the list of permitted services.

The regulator also introduced new requirements:

- Gradual increase of the authorized capital to T100 million.
- Debt-to-income ratio of 50% of borrower's total official income for consumer loans.
- Maximum effective interest rate of 56% applicable to online MFOs, which were also placed under the NBK regulatory umbrella.
- No charges for the issuance or servicing of loans and no penalties and fees for unsecured retail consumer loans that are 90 days past due or more.

The NBK developed criteria for creditworthiness and solvency, which will be binding for both second-tier banks and MFOs. The new two-step procedure involves the assessment of a borrower's solvency[25] as credit institutions are prohibited from issuing loans to individuals whose income is below the subsistence level. According to the NBK, this measure will reduce the economic incentives to issue unsecured loans, especially to low-income individuals. Next is the calculation of the borrower's debt ratio. These changes affected unsecured loans and are expected to benefit the development of the microfinance sector by diversifying MFOs' services and bringing more stability into their operations.

MFOs prepare their financial reporting as per the International Financial Reporting Standards (IFRS). They are not required to pass annual audits and publish their financial statements unless they are registered as joint-stock companies, which was allowed only from 2020.

---

[21] Law of the Republic of Kazakhstan dated 26 November 2012 "On Microfinance Activities."

[22] T20.2 million ($53,736 at the exchange rate of the NBK on 21 January 2020 [$1.00 = T375.91]). MCI was T2,525 in 2019.

[23] MFOs have been lobbying for permission to open accounts and engage in foreign exchange, but they were not allowed to do so. These services are closely associated with the lending process, so MFOs remain dependent on banks in this respect.

[24] T63.125 million or $167,926 (at the exchange rate of the NBK on 21 January 2020: T375.91)

[25] The client's solvency now takes into account the number of minor children in the family. Each child should have half the cost-of-living allowance, e.g., if the borrower has two children, his/her salary must be higher than T62,000, that is, 31.183 (the subsistence minimum approved for 2020) + (15 591.5 x 2)= 62,364. Credit institutions shall calculate the solvency of the client according to the formula $BI \geq SM + 0.5*SM*Nmc$; where BI = Borrower's income; SM = the subsistence minimum approved for the financial year specified by the Llw on the republican budget (e.g., in 2020 it was T31.183); Nmc = number of minor children in the family.

Prudential Requirements

In the beginning of 2020, the regulator has tightened[26] the prudential requirements for MFOs, which were initially introduced in 2016.[27] Table 26 lists these requirements and the changes in 2020.

Table 26: Microfinance Organizations Prudential Standards

Prudential Requirement	Level Required from 1 January 2016	New Level Required from 1 January 2020	Changes Introduced 30 May 2020[a]
Minimum authorized capital	T30 million	T100 million/ For the existing MFOs: T50 million from 1 July 2020; T70 million from 1 July 2021; T100 million from 1 July 2022	T100 million/ For the existing MFOs: T50 million from 1 January 2021; T70 million from 1 January 2022; T100 million from 1 January 2023
Minimum equity capital	T30 million	Same as for the authorized capital (see above)	Same as for the authorized capital (see above)
Capital adequacy k1	(Total equity/ Total assets) = at least 0.1	(Total equity/ (Assets + unsecured consumer loans) = at least 0.1	–
Single borrower risk k2 (Single borrower risk/ MFO total equity)	Up to 0.25	Up to 0.25	
Leverage ratio k3 (Total liabilities/ Total equity)[b]	Not more than 10	Not more than 10	

MFO = microfinance organization.

[a] Due to the state of emergency imposed in March 2020, the Agency made a decision (Resolution No.55 of the Board dated 30 May 2020) to postpone for 6 months the terms for increasing capital requirements for MFOs.
[b] In calculating the coefficient k3 for a credit partnership, the obligations of the national managing holdings and their subsidiaries in the agriculture sector are excluded from the total obligations of the credit partnership.

Source: The Law of the Republic of Kazakhstan "On Microfinance Organizations" as amended on 3 July 2019 and changes which were enforced from 1 January 2020.

The changes mainly affected prudential requirements related to capital: the minimum bar is gradually raised to T100 million by 2022 and capital adequacy calculation includes unsecured loans for an extra buffer. These measures are expected to facilitate the consolidation of the sector with the smaller players leaving or merging with/into others. At the start of 2020, more than half of the MFOs had a capital of less than T100 million.

---

[26] Prudential standard rates and others obligatory to observance by the organization performing microfinancial activities, regulations and limits, and the technique of their calculations approved by Resolution No. 192 of the Board of the NBK dated 14 November 2019.
[27] Resolution No. 382 of the Board of the NBK dated 24 December 2012: "On approval of prudential standards and other obligatory to observance by the microfinance organization of regulations and limits and techniques of their calculation and the forms and timing of reporting on their implementation" with changes.

Table 27: Microfinance Organization Sector Structure, by Size of Authorized Capital

Size of the Authorized Capital of MFOs as of January 2020 (T million)	Number of MFOs	Percentage of total number of MFOs (%)
< 50	81	41
50 – 100	39	20
100 – 500	55	28
500 – 1000	9	5
>= 1000	15	8

MFO = microfinance organization.

Source: Calculated using data from the National Bank of Kazakhstan/Agency.

Market Participants and Market Shares

There are almost 200 MFOs registered with the NBK, with the top three players accounting for 67% of aggregate assets and the top 10 players for 83% in 2019. The combined share of the remaining 189 MFOs is only 17%, with individual shares not exceeding 1%.

Table 28: Top 10 Microfinance Organizations, 2019

Ranking	Concentration	Share in Total Assets	Share in Total Loans	Share in Total Equity
1	Kazakhstan Loan Fund	42%	45%	34%
2	Toyota Financial Services	19%	19%	7%
3	OnlineKazFinance (Solva)	6%	6%	3%
4	Arnur Credit	6%	6%	5%
5	Urys	3%	3%	6%
6	Asian Credit Fund	2%	2%	2%
7	Shinhan Finance	2%	3%	5%
8	Regional Investment Center «Kyzyl-Orda»	2%	1%	3%
9	BNK Finance	1%	1%	3%
10	MC-Finance	1%	1%	0%
11-199	Remaining 189 MFOs	17%	13%	33%
Total		100%	100%	100%

Source: Calculated using data from the National Bank of Kazakhstan/Agency for Regulation and Development of the Financial Market.

The largest player accounting for 42% in total assets and 45% in total loans is the Kazakhstan Loan Fund (KMF). In 2019, KMF grew slower than the market (up by 14% of the assets; Table 29) with its share in total assets declining from 50% in 2018. Established in 1997, the company is probably the longest-existing MFO with a proven track record and a strong management team which has successfully steered the institution through crises. KMF is well-known locally and internationally, and is an active participant of Damu Fund and IFI-run MSME development programs.

The company that has demonstrated the quickest growth since 2018 is OnlineKazFinance (known as Solva and previously, MoneyMan), which jumped in the rankings from no. 16 in 2017 to no. 3 in 2019. It has outpaced the market, registering 35% and 242% growth versus the market's 6% and 38%, respectively (Table 29). Solva is the online lending platform. It sells "no hassle" 8-minute loans via smartphone or tablet devices to consumers and entrepreneurs for various purposes, including refinancing of existing loans.

Another champion that managed to double its assets in 2019 is BNK Finance, which moved up the ranks from no. 15 in 2018 to no. 9 in 2019. The company is a subsidiary of a larger group from the Republic of Korea and there is not much publicly available information about its operations apart from the reporting published by the NBK. Toyota Financial Services, Shinhan Finance, and MC-Finance also grew much quicker than the market: 95% for Toyota Financial Services and 71% for Shinhan Finance, while MC-Finance, which was set up only in late 2018, managed to grow into the tenth-largest company in just 1 year. The three companies, all relatively new in the market, specialize in auto-lending and are captive financial spin-offs of larger manufacturing and financial groups.

Table 29: Ranking of Microfinance Organizations

Change in Ranking 2017/2018/ 2019	Name of Microfinance Organization	Assets (T million)			Growth, Year on Year (%)		Percentage of Total (%)		
		2017	2018	2019	2018/ 2017	2019/ 2018	2017	2018	2019
1/1/1	Kazakhstan Loan Fund	123,336	129,229	147,592	5	14	51	50	42
2/2/2	Toyota Financial Services	32,560	35,454	69,121	9	95	13	14	19
16/7/3	OnlineKazFinance (Solva)	4,308	5,836	19,969	35%	242	2	2	6
3/3/4	Arnur Credit	13,291	14,771	19,925	11	35	5	6	6
4/4/5	Yrys	11,703	10,289	10,435	-12	1	5	4	3
5/6/6	Asian Credit Fund	5,221	5,824	7,717	12	33	2	2	2
8/7/7	Shinhan Finance	4,005	4,459	7,632	11	71	2	2	2
9/8/8	Regional Investment Center Kyzyl-Orda	3,274	4,214	5,451	29	29	1	2	2
15/9	BNK Finance	-	1,834	3,797	N/A	107	0	1	1
10	MC-Finance	-	-	3,335	N/A	N/A	0	0	1
Total		**242,170**	**256,516**	**355,217**	**6**	**38**	**100**	**100**	**100**

Source: Calculated using data from the National Bank of Kazakhstan/Agency for Regulation and Development of the Financial Market.

Arnur Credit, Yrys, and Asian Credit Fund moved one position down in the rankings. Arnur Credit and Asian Credit Fund grew by 35% and 33%, respectively, in 2019 in line with the market. Both companies are classical MFOs with the regional network of offices providing microloans to individuals and entrepreneurs. Both work with international financing institutions (IFIs). There is very little publicly available information about Yrys (1% growth) and Regional Financial Center Kyzyl-Orda (29% growth).

To sum up, in 2019, the quick market growth of almost 40% was fueled by new companies, particularly a technological MFO that provides quick loans online and MFOs selling auto-loans.

Financial Performance

At the end of 2019, the total assets of the MFO sector amounted to T355 billion, still quite small compared to the banking sector. The MFO sector's assets represent a tiny 1.3% of total banking sector assets. The MFO sector has grown actively over the past 3 years although the growth rate is slowing down: 49% in 2017, 36% in 2018, and 38% in 2019. The sector's loan portfolio is the largest asset, accounting for more than 80% of total assets and growing at about the same pace as the assets.

Table 30: Financial Performance: Aggregate Balance Sheet

Balance Sheet (T million)	2017	2018	2019
Loan portfolio	159,956	219,454	293,336
Total assets	188,480	256,516	355,217
Borrowed loans	121,202	168,449	n/a
Total liabilities	127,180	177,331	246,609
Total equity	61,301	79,184	108,608
Key ratios			
Growth of loans (%)	58	37	34
Growth of assets (%)	49	36	38
Loan portfolio/ Assets (%)	85	86	83
Borrowed loans / (total liabilities + total equity)	64	66	n/a
Total equity/ (total liabilities + total equity)	**33**	**31**	**31**

Source: Calculated using data from the National Bank of Kazakhstan/Agency for Regulation and Development of the Financial Market

Funding

The non-equity funding is mainly represented by loans as MFOs are non-deposit-taking institutions. Borrowings account for almost 70% of the total funding base (if total equity is included). Due to the absence of publicly available information, it is not possible to comment on the funding profile (maturity and currency).

Commercial sources of funding available to MFOs include IFIs and local banks. The rates of the tenge funding from IFIs range between 17% and 21%, and represents up to 77% of the entire debt funding of the sector.[28] Tenge funding from local banks is slightly cheaper and stands at 13%-14%; however, this is issued against collateral. There is also government funding, e.g., Yenbek program and MSME programs administered by the Damu Fund, but these programs either have a cap on the MFOs' end-borrower rate and/or have a long application review period which, coupled with the need of security, does not make it an appealing proposition. According to MFOs, it would help to set transparent eligibility criteria for Damu Fund financing such as a list of acceptable audit companies, minimum required performance indicators, and requirements to collateral and terms for consideration of the application. In 2018, six MFOs participated in the Damu Fund MSME programs, with less than 1% share in total financing value and 57% share in total number of issued loans. KMF was the largest participating MFO, accounting for more than 90% of the amounts channeled via MFOs. In 2017, several MFO subsidiaries of the NCE received funding under the Yenbek program administered by the Damu Fund and the programs administered by the ACC.

In 2020, MFOs were permitted to raise funding by the issuance of bonds in the stock market. Larger MFOs may be interested in this as a way to diversify their funding base. Institutionally they are more fit than smaller MFOs to comply with the requirements of the stock exchanges.

On aggregate, the sector is quite well capitalized with a total equity accounting for 31% of the consolidated assets.

Portfolio Quality

Compared to banks' portfolios, MFOs' loan portfolios have historically weathered crises better. One of the reasons is the greater granularity of their portfolios which spreads the risk over a greater population of borrowers. In addition, micro and small businesses are usually quicker to adapt their operations to the changing macroeconomic reality, which helps to minimize their losses.

According to the NBK, at the end of 2019, total overdue loans of the MFO sector accounted for 7.6% of total loans. Most of the overdues (7.4% of the total 7.6%) were in the retail portfolio[29] which represents the bulk (98%) of loans. Corporate loans issued by MFOs account for a negligible 2% and most of them are standard. Provision coverage of loans past due for 90 days or more is 73% at the end of 2018.

Profit and loss reflects the structure of the balance sheet with most of the income generated by the loan portfolio: interest income on loans represents 78% of total income in 2019 (82% in 2018). This structure may change going forward as MFOs are allowed to provide additional services starting 2020, which will diversify their income structure. Portfolio yield is slightly over 30% and after the cost of borrowings of about 16%, the implied net interest margin is about 23%.[30] Cost–income ratio is high (73%), signaling that the cost of running this business is quite high so MFOs always need to explore new ways of increasing operating efficiency, and technology may be the answer.

---

[28]   Association of Microfinance Organizations.
[29]   Most of these loans include loans to households for business purposes.
[30]   The calculation is based on the available MFO statistics collected and published by the NBK/Agency.

Table 31: Loan Portfolio Quality
(%)

Loan Portfolio	2017	2018	2019
Corporate loans	2.0	1.8	1.9
- standard	1.8	1.6	1.7
- overdue	0.1	0.2	0.2
< 30	0.0	0.0	0.1
31-60	0.0	0.0	0.0
61-90	0.0	0.0	0.0
> 90	0.1	0.1	0.1
Retail loans	98.0	98.2	98.1
- standard	92.4	92.3	90.7
- overdue	5.7	5.9	7.4
< 30	1.6	1.7	2.2
31-60	0.9	0.7	0.9
61-90	0.4	0.4	0.5
> 90	2.8	3.1	3.9
Total loans	100.0	100.0	100.0
Loan loss reserves or loans past due more than 90 days	69%	73%	n/a

Source: Calculated using data from the National Bank of Kazakhstan/Agency for Regulation and Development of the Financial Market.

Table 32: Financial Performance: Aggregate Profit and Loss
(T million unless otherwise stated)

Profit and Loss	2017	2018	2019
Interest income	45,782	67,073	89,170
- Interest income on loans	42,841	62,449	80,574
Total income	50,786	76,080	103,186
Interest expense	15,403	22,735	30,063
Allocation to reserves	2,678	5,892	11,149
Operating expense including	14,119	16,705	22,603
- Salary	12,027	14,097	17,017
Other	6,522	10,022	10,997
Total expenses	38,722	55,355	74,812
Corporate income tax	2,260	4,033	5,209
Net income	9,803	16,691	23,165

continued on next page

Table 32 *continued*

Profit and Loss	2017	2018	2019
Key ratios			
Portfolio yield	33%	33%	31%
Cost of borrowings	16%	16%	n/a
Net interest margin	23%	23%	23%
Cost/income	76%	73%	73%
OSS (self-sufficient ratio)	131%	137%	138%
Allocation to LLR/Total expenses	7%	11%	15%
Return on average assets	6%	8%	8%
Return on average equity	18%	24%	25%

LLR = loan loss reserves, OSS = operational self-sufficiency (that measures revenues over the main expenses).

Source: Calculated using data from the National Bank of Kazakhstan.

Allocation to loan loss reserves as a proportion of operating expenses is on the rise. From 7% in 2017, it went up to 11% in 2018 and 15% in 2019, reflecting higher pressures on profitability from the loan portfolio quality. Return on average assets and return on average equity stood at 8% and 25%, respectively, in 2018, and at 8% and 24%, respectively, in 2019. Forty-one MFOs closed 2019 with a net loss,[31] which has likely exerted certain downward pressure on net profitability margins.

Portfolio Structure

Portfolio Structure by Type of Borrower, Purpose, and Security

The MFO sector portfolio amounted to T389 billion in 2019,[32] growing by 36% in value and by 9% in number from 2018. The slower growth by number and quicker growth by volume suggests the growth of the average loan size, which increased from T588,107 to T733,193 in 2018.

Consumer loans to individuals (63% in 2019, 57% in 2018) and business loans to individual entrepreneurs (26% in 2019, 32% in 2018) were the largest items in the portfolio structure. Consumer loans to individual entrepreneurs and business loans to corporates accounted for 9% and 2%, respectively, in 2019 (9% and 1%, respectively, in 2018). The proportions are about the same if measured by the number of loans.

In 2019, the growth of loans to individuals (16% in 2019, 51% in 2018) was quicker in both value and number than the growth of loans to corporates (-3% in 2019, 18% in 2018), as shown in Table 34.

---

[31]   As per the information of the Association of MFOs: https://www.amfok.kz/sections/Statistics.
[32]   This section is based on the portfolio data of the First Credit Bureau which differs from the data of the NBK.

Table 33: Structure of Loans Issued by Microfinance Organizations

Type of Loans	T million		Number of Loans		% in Total Value		% in Total Number		Growth in %		Average Loan Size (T)		Growth of the Average Loan Size
	2018	2019	2018	2019	2018	2019	2018	2019	of value	of number	2018	2019	
Consumer loans to individuals	162,848	245,360	324,784	375,616	57	63	67	71	51	16	501,404	653,220	30
Secured	59,050	99,830	18,711	23,448	21	26	4	4	69	25	3,155,898	4,257,506	35
Unsecured	103,798	145,530	306,073	352,168	36	37	63	66	40	15	339,128	413,240	22
Consumer loans to IPs	26,730	34,251	22,765	18,689	9	9	5	4	28	-18	1,174,171	1,832,682	56
Secured	18,423	26,414	11,035	11,128	6	7	2	2	43	1	1,669,506	2,373,652	42
Unsecured	8,307	7,837	11,730	7,561	3	2	2	1	-6	-36	708,184	1,036,503	46
Business loans to IPs	92,154	102,131	136,963	136,024	32	26	28	26	11	-1	672,839	750,831	12
Secured	56,394	74,022	67,803	85,100	20	19	14	16	31	26	831,733	869,824	5
Unsecured	35,760	28,109	69,160	50,924	13	7	14	10	-21	-26	517,062	551,979	7
Business loans to corporates	3,526	7,620	532	721	1	2	0	0%	116	36%	6,627,820	10,568,655	59
Secured	3,277	7,251	499	648	1	2	0	0	121	30	6,567,134	11,189,815	70
Unsecured	249	369	33	73	0	0	0	0	48	121	7,545,455	5,054,795	-33
Total	285,258	389,362	485,044	531,050	100	100	100	100	36	9	588,107	733,193	25

IP = individual entrepreneurs.

Source: First Credit Bureau.

Individuals can engage in entrepreneurial activities, whether registered (as an individual entrepreneur, peasant or farm enterprise) or unregistered. Registration is not required for entrepreneurs who do not have employees, sell services only to individuals, or sell agriculture produce from their own households. Such entrepreneurs pay single aggregate payment equal to 1 MCI / 0.5 MCI depending on the location of their business. This replaces a number of taxes and allows them to remain within the social security network.

The bulk of loans (72% of the value and 74% of number) were issued for consumer purposes (Table 36). The average size of a consumer loan grew by 30%, from T545,471 to T709,124. The practice in some MFOs is to issue business loans but document them as for consumers[33] so some consumer loans may include loans issued for business purposes. Usually, consumer loans to individuals are issued only if the income is proved; the share of such loans in classical MFOs is not significant.

The breakdown of loans into secured and unsecured (Table 37) indicates that while they are roughly split by value, unsecured loans dominate by number, accounting for 77% in 2019. Unsecured loans include group loans to microentrepreneurs and individual loans secured by third-party guarantee. In case of default, the law provides the lender with recourse related to the borrower and/or guarantor's income such as the arrest of accounts and deduction of any bank account balances toward the repayment.

Portfolio Structure by Gender

There are generally no gender-sensitive issues when it comes to access to finance in Kazakhstan. This is confirmed by a review of the MFO portfolio by gender which showed that women and men have equal access to finance, with women accounting for over half of loans, in terms of value (Table 4). The Committee on Statistics show women as engaged in business leadership, with about 43% of MSMEs in Kazakhstan being women-led in 2018.

There are no gender-specific national development programs for MSMEs as all programs provide equal access to men and women qualifying the program criteria. There are two noncommercial organizations— the Council of Business Women at the NCE and the Association of Women in Business—that were set up to consolidate and strengthen women's role in business and make women-led entrepreneurship more visible.

Among IFIs, there is the Women in Business program launched in 2016 by the ERBD, which is implemented jointly with the Damu Fund and other participating financial institutions and MFOs. Women can benefit from financing as well as skills training and coaching under this program.

Portfolio Structure by Region and Urban–Rural Distribution

At the end of 2018, the portfolio of the MFO sector was concentrated in the cities of Almaty and Shymkent, and in the South Kazakhstan region.

The concentration of MFOs in the large cities is confirmed by the Association of MFOs, which found that in 2019, 90 MFOs accounting for as much as 80% of the aggregate loan portfolio were registered in Almaty. The combined share of 152 MFOs registered in Almaty, Nur-Sultan, Karaganda region, and Shymkent in the aggregate loan portfolio is 92%.

---

[33]   As understood, the reason for this is that the consumer loan requires less documentation.

Overview of the Microfinance Sector

Table 34: Microfinance Organizations Loan Portfolio by Individuals and Corporates, 2018–2019

Item	T million		Number of Loans		% in Total Value		% in Total Number		Growth		Average Loan Size, T		Growth of the Average Loan Size
	2018	2019	2018	2019	2018	2019	2018	2019	of value	of number	2018	2019	
Individuals	162,848	245,360	324,784	375,616	57%	63%	67%	71%	51%	16%	501,404	653,220	30%
Corporates	122,410	144,002	160,260	155,434	43%	37%	33%	29%	18%	-3%	763,821	926,451	21%
Total	**285,258**	**389,362**	**485,044**	**531,050**	**100%**	**100%**	**100%**	**100%**	**36%**	**9%**	**588,107**	**733,193**	**25%**

Source: First Credit Bureau.

Table 35: Microfinance Organizations' Portfolio Structure by Loan Purpose

Item	T million		Number of Loans		% in Total Value		% in Total Number		Growth		Average Loan Size, T		Growth of the Average Loan Size
	2018	2019	2018	2019	2018	2019	2018	2019	of value	of number	2018	2019	
Business loans	95,680	109,751	137,495	136,745	34%	28%	28%	26%	15%	-1%	695,880	802,596	15%
Consumer loans	189,578	279,611	347,549	394,305	66%	72%	72%	74%	47%	13%	545,471	709,124	30%
Total	**285,258**	**389,362**	**485,044**	**531,050**	**100%**	**100%**	**100%**	**100%**	**36%**	**9%**	**588,107**	**733,193**	**25%**

Source: First Credit Bureau.

Table 36: Microfinance Organizations' Loan Collateral Structure

Item	T million		Number of Loans		% in Total Value		% in Total Number		Growth		Average Loan Size, T		Growth of the Average Loan Size
	2018	2019	2018	2019	2018	2019	2018	2019	of value	of number	2018	2019	
Secured	137,144	207,517	98,048	120,324	48%	53%	20%	23%	51%	23%	1,398,743	1,724,652	23%
Unsecured	148,114	181,845	386,996	410,726	52%	47%	80%	77%	23%	6%	382,727	442,740	16%
Total	**285,258**	**389,362**	**485,044**	**531,050**	**100%**	**100%**	**100%**	**100%**	**36%**	**9%**	**588,107**	**733,193**	**25%**

Source: First Credit Bureau.

Table 37: Issuing Loans to Microfinance Organizations by Gender, 2018–2019
(%)

Item	Q2 2018	Q3 2018	Q4 2018	Q1 2019	Q2 2019	Q3 2019	Q4 2019
Loans by value							
Women	55.4	55.3	56	55.1	55.4	55.1	54.6
Men	44.6	44.7	44	44.9	44.6	44.9	45.4
Loans by number							
Women	62.4	63.6	61.4	59.4	62.0	62.4	63.6
Men	37.6	36.4	38.6	40.6	38	37.6	36.4

Note: Available statistics were used for analysis; statistics were not published regularly or in the public domain.

Source: First Credit Bureau.

Table 38: Loan Portfolio of Microfinance Organizations by Region

Region	T million		Share	
	2017	2018	2017	2018
Almaty City	129,752	180,861	76.3%	78.8%
Shymkent City	0	23,383	0.0%	10.2%
Nur-Sultan City	5,711	6,585	3.4%	2.9%
Kyzylorda	2,497	4,699	1.5%	2.0%
East Kazakhstan	1,667	2,106	1.0%	0.9%
Almaty	1,274	1,749	0.7%	0.8%
Aktobe	1,867	1,344	1.1%	0.6%
Karaganda	1,154	1,318	0.7%	0.6%
Kostanay	932	1,220	0.5%	0.5%
Mangystau	827	1,167	0.5%	0.5%
North Kazakhstan	1,293	1,132	0.8%	0.5%
Zhambyl	909	1,008	0.5%	0.4%
Turkestan	0	819	0.0%	0.4%
Atyrau	651	789	0.4%	0.3%
Akmola	901	687	0.5%	0.3%
West Kazakhstan	713	654	0.4%	0.3%
Pavlodar	62	52	0.0%	0.0%
South Kazakhstan	19,901	0	11.7%	0.0%
Total	**170,110**	**229,574**	**100%**	**100%**

Source: Government of Kazakhstan, Ministry of National Economy, Committee on Statistics.

There is no publicly available information on the number of rural borrowers served by the microfinance sector. The information by the amount of outstanding loans in 2012–2016 indicates that MFOs mainly lend in urban areas (94.3%), which is not surprising as Kazakhstan is not an exception to the global urbanization trend with most of the economically active population migrating to large cities for better employment opportunities.

Table 39: Microfinance Organizations' Portfolio Structure, Urban versus Rural

	2012	2013	2014	2015	2016
Loans Disbursement (T million)	**238,507**	**197,789**	**212,069**	**257,280**	**411,659**
Urban area	220,228	174,868	185,890	235,095	388,230
Rural area	18,279	22,921	26,179	22,184	23,428
Urban area (%)	92.3	88.4	87.7	91.4	94.3
Rural area (%)	7.7	11.6	12.3	8.6	5.7

Source: Government of Kazakhstan, Ministry of National Economy, Committee on Statistics.

The share of loans in rural areas in Kazakhstan (5.7%) is much lower than in other regions globally (62% in Eastern Europe and Central Asia).[34] Several factors need to be taken into view when considering these numbers. First, the data cover only MFO portfolios, not banks, which also serve both rural and urban borrowers. Second, as a result of the urbanization trend in Kazakhstan, the population left in the rural areas, if bankable, takes smaller loans. Third, larger corporates operating in rural areas are normally booked on the balances of MFO headquarters and banks to comply with the prudential norms and as such are not recorded or reflected in the regional data.

Average Microloan Size

The average microloan size in 2019 increased by 25%, from T588,107 ($1,400) to T733,193 ($1,700). The breakdown of the aggregate portfolio by segment indicates that the average loan size has increased across the board, with the exception of unsecured loans to corporates, which went down by 33%, from T7.5 million to T5.1 million. The biggest increase in loan size was in the secured loans to corporates, where the average loan size grew by 70%, from T6.6 million ($15,700) to T11.2 million ($26,600). Despite this, loans to corporates represent negligible shares both in value and number. Average consumer loan to individual entrepreneurs also grew significantly—by 42% of secured loans and by 46% of unsecured loans while the same loans for businesses grew only 5% and 7%, respectively. The average size of a consumer loan to individuals also increased by 30%.

34 MIX. *Global Outreach & Financial Performance Benchmark Report – 2017–2018.* https://content.centerforfinancialinclusion.org/wp-content/uploads/sites/2/2021/07/MIXMarket_GlobalOutreachFinancialBenchmarkReport_2017-2018.pdf.

Table 40: Structure of the Microfinance Organizations' Loan Portfolio and Average Loan Size

Type of Loans	T milion		Number of Loans		% in Total Value		% in Total Number		Growth		Average Loan Size, T		Growth of the Average Loan Size
	2018	2019	2018	2019	2018	2019	2018	2019	of value	of number	2018	2019	
Consumer loans to individuals	162,848	245,360	324,784	375,616	57%	63%	67%	71%	51%	16%	501,404	653,220	30%
Secured	59,050	99,830	18,711	23,448	21%	26%	4%	4%	69%	25%	3,155,898	4,257,506	35%
Unsecured	103,798	145,530	306,073	352,168	36%	37%	63%	66%	40%	15%	339,128	413,240	22%
Consumer loans to IPs	26,730	34,251	22,765	18,689	9%	9%	5%	4%	28%	-18%	1,174,171	1,832,682	56%
Secured	18,423	26,414	11,035	11,128	6%	7%	2%	2%	43%	1%	1,669,506	2,373,652	42%
Unsecured	8,307	7,837	11,730	7,561	3%	2%	2%	1%	-6%	-36%	708,184	1,036,503	46%
Business loans to IPs	92,154	102,131	136,963	136,024	32%	26%	28%	26%	11%	-1%	672,839	750,831	12%
Secured	56,394	74,022	67,803	85,100	20%	19%	14%	16%	31%	26%	831,733	869,824	5%
Unsecured	35,760	28,109	69,160	50,924	13%	7%	14%	10%	-21%	-26%	517,062	551,979	7%
Business loans to corporates	3,526	7,620	532	721	1%	2%	0%	0%	116%	36%	6,627,820	10,568,655	59%
Secured	3,277	7,251	499	648	1%	2%	0%	0%	121%	30%	6,567,134	11,189,815	70%
Unsecured	249	369	33	73	0%	0%	0%	0%	48%	121%	7,545,455	5,054,795	-33%
Total	285,258	389,362	485,044	531,050	100%	100%	100%	100%	36%	9%	588,107	733,193	25%

IP = individual entrepreneurs.

Source: First Credit Bureau.

As the cap on maximum loan amount has been increased in 2020 from T20.2 million ($53,736) to T63.125 million ($167,926), the average loan sizes are expected to continue increasing. MFOs will need to adapt their technologies and train staff to serve more borrowers and provide larger loan amounts.

The average loan size can also be expressed as a percentage of the gross national income (GNI) per capita to allow a better comparison between countries. The assumption is that the smaller the loan size is as a percentage of the GNI per capita, the poorer are the clients served by MFOs. The average loan size as a percentage of the GNI per capita in Kazakhstan was 17.4% in 2018. This is better than the 2% in Turkey and 12% in France but is lower than 22% in Romania and 24% in Belgium. The highest average loan size as a proportion of GNI per capita is in Hungary and Poland, 146% and 107%, respectively.

Products and Interest Rates

The product proposition and pricing of each MFO depend on the resources at hand. Classical and state/municipal MFOs offer a range of products tailored for the needs of corporate and retail borrowers. In addition to the standard working-capital loans, for example, some MFOs offer agriculture loans with repayment terms that take into account seasonality. Other MFOs offer group loans where loans are issued to entrepreneurs who know and trust each other enough such that their loans are secured by their mutual guarantees. Some MFOs also offer nonfinancial services (training, seminars, coaching, etc.) in an effort to increase the outcomes of financial products by improving clients' financial management, entrepreneurship, and business development skills. Captive MFOs typically sell only auto-loans, which can vary in maturity, while online platforms mostly sell consumer loans with a maturity of up to a year.

On average, microloan rates ranged from 22.6% to 38.4% in 2019. As of 1 February 2020, under the Yenbek program, all MFOs affiliated with the NCE have disbursed T2.05 billion. Funds received under this program through the Agrarian Credit Corporation (ACC) were issued to the final borrowers, i.e., unemployed and self-employed, at 6% interest rate per annum, mainly to allow them to start a business.

Interest rates of short-term loans for individuals are higher than for legal entities, but for long-term loans, individuals enjoy a lower interest rate than legal entities. Given the small share of MFO financing of legal entities, the current indicator cannot be characterized as a trend.

Table 41: Weighted Average Interest Rates of Microfinance Organizations, 2016–2019

	2016	2017	2018	2019
Loans to individuals				
short term	29.4	23.9	28.0	n/a
long term	19.4	21.3	24.3	n/a
Loans to legal entities				
short term	35.8	27.5	22.6	n/a
long term	35.2	38.3	38.4	n/a

Note: These are the indicated nominal rates.
Source: Association of Microfinance Organizations of Kazakhstan.

MFOs mainly issue short-term loans for working capital/consumer goals. Loans for fixed assets and with a maturity of over 1 year are insignificant in the total share of loans issued.

Table 42: Small and Medium-Sized Enterprise Lending: Microfinance Organizations Product Card

Interviewed MFOs	Minimum	Maximum	Average
Interest rate (%)	19	45	30-36
Maximum term (month)	1-12	36-60	9
Maximum credit amount (T'000)	5	20,000	1,000

MFO = microfinance organization.

Source: Calculated using data from corporate websites and data provided by MFOs. Excludes government programs.

Conclusions

The microfinance market in Kazakhstan occupies a small share of the financing market. The total loan portfolio of MFOs at the end of 2019 was only 2.1% of the portfolio of the banking sector. MFOs cater to the needs of a different client segment by offering loans that are, on average, smaller than those offered by banks.

In 2019, MFO sector growth was fueled to some extent by consumption as demonstrated by the higher growth of auto-lending and online platforms. The market share of classical business-oriented MFOs has shrunk, and their growth rate has been lower than the average market growth. There are several reasons for this:

- The technology-driven MFOs with their quicker and paperless processes have an advantage over traditional MFOs, especially among the younger generation of borrowers.
- In 2019, the Government of Kazakhstan launched the auto-lending program at subsidized rates to support the local auto-manufacturing sector. This explains the growth of MFOs specialized in auto-lending.
- The greater indebtedness of MSME borrowers constrains the growth of classical MFOs.

The requirement to increase MFO capitalization to T100 million by 2022 will wipe out many smaller MFOs, facilitate sector consolidation, and decrease competition. As of 1 January 2020, 39% of MFOs did not have the authorized capital T100 million (Table 27).

From 2020, MFOs will be able to provide more services in addition to microlending, but it remains to be seen whether these services will allow them to effectively diversify their income base. The services on opening of accounts and foreign exchange operations, which MFOs had been lobbying for already for some time and which can make their services more comprehensive, were not included in the list of permitted services.

5 Recommendations

Globally, microfinance is sometimes misunderstood or poorly perceived by the public and even economists. The cases of over-indebtedness of its clients and MFOs' excessive profits have earned criticism for the sector. Such cases have revealed the danger of unchecked microfinancing and the impact it can have on its clients. From 2010 to 2013, self-regulatory measures have been developed and improved, demonstrating the MFOs' willingness to professionalize the sector.[35]

During this period, microfinance entered a phase of professionalization and institutional strengthening. The transformation consisted of three parts: diversification of investments, expansion of new technologies, and innovative use and development of financial and nonfinancial services. An assessment of the impact of microfinance revealed that the sector not only contributes to access to credit, but to health, agriculture, education, energy, and housing services as well. MFOs play a significant role in supporting the social and financial inclusion of the most vulnerable clients.

Extensive international experience in the microfinance sector can be useful for many emerging markets, including Kazakhstan's MSMEs. Recent surveys of MSME financing in global markets note that the greatest impacts on financing for MSMEs, to date, are policy and regulation, external environment, technology, and MSME capacity building and funding, to which the microfinance sector contributes significantly.

Microfinance Market Development

This report cannot be considered a comprehensive and extensive market research, but it provides a diagnostic look at the problems and most important aspects for the development of the microfinance market in Kazakhstan and the professionalization of its stakeholders. Based on the conclusions of this study, the following recommendations are made:

Table 43: Recommendations for Microfinance Market Development in Kazakhstan

	Areas Being Addressed	Recommendations	Priority
1. Regulatory Environment			
1.1	Encourage competition in the microfinance market.	Facilitate the entry of new agents offering financial services for MSMEs and/or contribute to the maturity of existing agents.	low
1.2	Focus the MFO sector on a segment not being served by banks.	Motivate MFOs to serve rural and remote regions and develop products for low-income business clients.	high

continued on next page

---

35 Convergences. 2019. *Microfinance Barometer 2019*. https://www.convergences.org/wp-content/uploads/2019/09/Microfinance-Barometer-2019_web-1.pdf.

Table 43 *continued*

	Areas Being Addressed	Recommendations	Priority
1.3	Build MFO institutional capacity.	Assist MFOs in product development and improvement of lending conditions, largely depending on funding available on the market and hedging instruments.	high
1.4	Develop risk management standards for MFOs.	Gradually introduce risk management standards for the sector to improve MFO risk management practices.	medium
1.5	Promote MFO institutional sustainability.	Foster MFOs to develop their institutional sustainability respect rights and protect clients' interests.	medium
1.6	Expand the range of MFO services.	With the growth of market maturity, expand the legislative list of services of MFOs to include collection of small deposits of MFO clients, insurance, transfers, and nonfinancial services. The regulator may introduce different types of licenses for various activities permitted for MFOs. Prudential requirements can also be adapted to the sets of services provided by MFO.	medium
1.7	Improve legal framework for entrepreneurship	Eliminate legislative imperfections regarding corporate bankruptcy and protection of the rights of entrepreneurs.	medium
2. Market Infrastructure			
2.1	MSME statistics on performance: key indicators	MSME statistics should be significantly improved through better indicators, regular assessment, and more details from the regions. A set of key indicators should be defined for MSME development and supported by the national statistics agency.	high
2.2	MSMEs' financial inclusion: key assessment indicators	Set key assessment indicators for the national program on the financial inclusion development of MSMEs can be effective for market development.	high
2.3	Financial inclusion development: increasing access to finance	Facilitate internet penetration growth, especially in rural areas.	medium
2.4	MSMEs' financial literacy and/or transparency	Raise the legal and financial literacy of business owners and managers, and increase the transparency of enterprises.	medium
2.5	MFO statistics on performance: specific industry indicators	Data collection, statistics on MFOs activities and their analysis need to be improved to take into account specifics of microfinance activities such as the number of clients and issued loans; and indicators of financial and operational efficiency including staff performance, coverage by region, female entrepreneurship, rural borrowers, etc. The key performance indicators of MFOs should be set at the national level.	high
2.6	MFO statistics: social impact	Establish an assessment of MFOs' social impact and clients' rights protection based on international practices for market development.	high
2.7	MFO: support development of digital technologies and fintech in financial services	Stimulate the development of digital services and financial technology for use in national customer databases (credit bureaus, population income databases, etc.) and allow the use of advanced scoring tools to assess customers' creditworthiness.	high

continued on next page

Table 43 *continued*

	Areas Being Addressed	Recommendations	Priority
3. Specific Support Measures			
3.1	MFO funding	The cost and accessibility of funds for MFOs have a strong impact on their ability to lend to MSMEs. Providing credit lines and guarantees will allow MFOs to fund more MSMEs at a reduced cost. Increasing access to local currency funding will eliminate significant hedging risk for MFOs and enable them to offer MSMEs longer-maturing loans in the local currency. These measures will benefit MSME borrowers hit by the crisis and in need of restructuring to pay their obligations.	high
3.2	Assist classical MFOs with information technology (IT) and technology audits.	Assist the big classical MFOs with IT and technology audits to help them understand which areas of their process can be optimized in terms of time, cost, and efficiency to make them more competitive. The audit results will help them with the selection of the appropriate technology. Use case studies of successful technology-based institutions like Tinkoff Bank.	high
3.3	Staff training for MFOs	Continue the assistance especially in the area of risk management given the worsening macroeconomic situation and the COVID-19 impact on financial institutions' loan portfolios.	medium
3.4	Special support for MFOs and lending programs	Create special support programs for microfinance market participants that introduce innovative digital services, have social impact, promote energy-saving technologies, and finance women-led entrepreneurship.	medium

COVID-19 = coronavirus disease, MFO = microfinance organization, MSME = micro, small, and medium enterprise.

Source: Study author's recommendations.

Technical Assistance

Technical support measures facilitating sustainable market development can be provided by state agencies and development institutions. Technical support can be broken down into general events for the sector and individual support for specific MFOs. The range of support measures are broad: Table 44 lists those most demanded by MFOs to address market development challenges.

On top of training, technical assistance, such as consulting projects that strengthen the organization's key functions (risk management, digitalization, underwriting, etc.) tailored to individual MFOs, will also be in demand. For the design of such assistance, it is recommended to do individual surveys of organizations.

Table 44: Training for Microfinance Organizations

	Support Measures	Audience	Most Demanded	Form of Delivery	
				Sector	Individual
1	**MFO personnel training**				
	Microbusiness borrower's financial statement and creditworthiness assessment	LS	X	X	X
	SME's financial statement and creditworthiness assessment	LS, RM	X	X	X
	Development of loan products	RM, MM, TM		X	
	MFO's credit risk management	RM, LS	X		X
	MFO's operational risk management	RM, MM		X	
	Financial risk management	RM, MM		X	
	Strategic planning: strategic sessions and plan development	TM, MM	X		X
	MFO strategic marketing	MS			X
	MFO sales management	LS, MM, MS	X	X	X
	MFO's underwriting system	LS, RM, MM		X	X
	Overdue debt management (hard and soft collection)	RM, LS		X	
	Microfinance business digitalization	ITS, MM, RM	X	X	X
	MFO operations' social impact assessment	ITS, MM, RM		X	
	Soft skills training: negotiations, conflict management, emotions and stress management	LS, MM			X
2	**MSME client training**				
	Financial literacy	MSME clients using the infrastructure of MFOs with focus on remote regions			X
	Using modern online services (financial, state)				X
	How to start a business in Kazakhstan: types of entrepreneurships, registration, bookkeeping, taxation, business regulation, government inspections				X
	Industry seminars: crop production, animal husbandry, services rendering, etc.			X	

ITS = information technology staff, LS = loan specialist, MFO = microfinance organization, MM = middle management, MS = marketing specialist, MSME = micro, small, and medium enterprise, RM = risk manager, SME = small and medium-sized enterprise, TM = top management.

Source: Study author's recommendations.

Appendixes

APPENDIX 1

Participating Microfinance Organizations

Table A1: List of Interviewed Microfinance Organizations

No.	Organization	Contact Person/ Interviewee	Date
1	Association of Microfinance Organizations of Kazakhstan	Erbol Omarkhanov, Director	3 Feb 2020
2	First Credit Bureau	Nurgalieva Asem Bolatzhanovna Executive Director	4 Feb 2020
3	Damu Entrepreneurship Development Fund JSC	Nazym Kydrali, Head of the APEX Department	4 Feb 2020
		Ablyakhad Baltaev New Head of the APEX Department	5 Mar 2020
4	National Chamber of Entrepreneurs of the Republic of Kazakhstan (Atameken)	CEO of the regional Atamaken MFOs	20 Feb 2020
	Almaty Region		
5	Microfinance organization «KMF» LLP (#35)	Saule Ibraeva, Deputy Head of the Credit Department; Asem Egizbekova, Deputy Manager, Business Development Department; Akzhelen Moldabekova, Manager of the Legal Department.	5 Feb 2020
6	Asian Credit Fund LLP (#6)	Zhakupova Zhanna Bolathanovna	4 Feb 2020
7	Shinhan Finance LLP (#7)	Oh Yuong Kyo, Executive Director Jung Young Il, General manager	19 Feb 2020
8	Toyota Financial Services LLP (#2)	Konev Stanislav, Finance Manager Saule Alimzhanova Corporate Reporting and Treasury Manager, Finance Department	19 Feb 2020
9	OnlineKazFinance LLP (#4)	Marat Bekzhanov, CEO	17 Feb 2020
	South Region		
10	Arnur Credit LLP (#3)	Raushan Kurbanaliyeva, CEO	28 Feb 2020
11	Yrys LLP (#5)	Daniyar Aryngazin, CEO Saule Tulendivea, Deputy Director	28 Feb 2020

continued on next page

Table A1 *continued*

No.	Organization	Contact Person/ Interviewee	Date
12	GFM LLP (#15)	Makhsat Dauletaliyev, CEO Yerdos Dauletbay, Chairman of the Board of Directors	26 Feb 2020
14	Taraz LLP (#14)	Nurlybek Isaev, CEO	27 Feb 2020
15	Atameken Taraz LLP (#24)	Samat Kosaliev, CEO	27 Feb 2020
	North Region		
16	MiG Credit Astana LLP (#16)	Kurmanov Askhat Maratovich	12 Feb 2020
17	Bereke LLP (#11)	Zhumagul Hayrlybayeva	12 Feb 2020 conference call
	West Region		
18	Atyrau Microfinance Center LLP (#30)	Kamalov Renuar Bizhanovich	14 Feb 2020

CEO = chief executive officer, MFO = microfinance organization.

Note: Figures in parentheses indicate the number of positions by assets reported by the National Bank of Kazakhstan as of 1 October 2019.

Source: Author's data.

APPENDIX 2
Statistical Data

Table A2.1: Main Indicators of Small Enterprises

Year	Number of Active Subjects ('000 units)			Number of Employed ('000 people)			Output Production (T billion)		
	Legal Entities	IE	FE	legal entities	IE	FE	legal entities	IE	FE
2009	60.6	428.4	170.2	551.3	874.4	465.8	1,270.7	371.2	402.0
2010	66.5	416.1	170.3	746.2	710.6	425.5	1,673.5	495.1	345.7
2011	64.5	589.6	183.0	539.3	771.9	426.5	1,445.2	675.1	586.4
2012	62.9	573.6	164.9	500.6	831.4	375.8	1,546.4	754.4	549.3
2013	61.1	660.3	158.6	527.5	990.7	346.9	1,871.1	949.8	734.4
2014	74.8	694.7	152.7	849.0	1,136.0	309.4	8,007.3	972.7	786.1
2015	175.7	882.8	181.2	1,185.2	1,360.3	286.5	10,200.1	1,518.2	904.5
2016	189.6	813.5	180.8	1,249.3	1,288.2	276.4	13,568.5	1,511.7	1,043.8
2017	208.7	747.1	187.5	1,301.8	1,240.9	286.0	16,488.0	1,554.7	1,152.5
2018	231.3	809.1	198.3	1,351.9	1,315.2	280.5	18,272.3	1,765.0	1,317.4
2019	260.9	855.9	213.5						

FE = peasant or farmer enterprises, IE = individual entrepreneurs.

Note: For 2014–2018, *The Entrepreneur Code of the Republic of Kazakhstan* dated 29 October 2015 no. 375-V used the average number of employees as a criterion to define small and medium-sized enterprises for state statistical purposes.
Source: Government of Kazakhstan, Ministry of National Economy, Committee on Statistics.

Table A2.2: Contribution of Micro, Small and Medium Enterprises to Gross Domestic Product by Region, 2015–Q3 2019
(%)

Region	2015	2016	2017	2018	Q3 2019
South Kazakhstan	20.2	22.9	21.9	–	–
Nur-Sultan City	46.0	57.4	54.4	48.6	54,2
Almaty City	29.1	33.7	35.3	40.1	41.0
North Kazakhstan	23.9	24.4	25.4	29.7	38.0
West Kazakhstan	39.9	41.9	40.1	36.0	36.9
Almaty region	25.1	26.9	26.4	32.0	31.2
Republic of Kazakhstan	**24.9**	**26.8**	**26.8**	**28.4**	**29.5**
Kostanay	21.8	23.2	25.1	29.4	28.7
Akmola	25.6	26.1	25.1	30.8	27.5

continued on next page

Table A2.2 *continued*

Region	2015	2016	2017	2018	Q3 2019
Shymkent City	-	-	-	25.6	27.4
Mangistau	19.9	22.9	15.6	16.8	23.9
Atyrau	14.2	11.8	16.8	18.7	20.8
Zhambyl	19.9	19.8	18.8	20.9	20.5
Turkestan	-	-	-	19.5	20.4
Aktobe	22.1	19.4	18.3	20.7	20.4
East Kazakhstan	15.4	16.9	15.7	18.0	18.3
Pavlodar	19.7	15.1	17.4	16.2	16.8
Karaganda	12.7	12.1	12.7	17.2	16.0
Kyzylorda	13.5	13.2	14.2	16.9	15.4

Source: Government of Kazakhstan, Ministry of National Economy, Committee on Statistics.

Table A2.3: Population by Region

Region	2017		2018		2019	
	People	%	People	%	People	%
The Republic of Kazakhstan	18,157,337	100.0	18,395,567	100.0	18,632,169	100.0
Almaty region	2,017,277	11.1	2,038,934	11.1	2,055,651	11.0
Turkestan	1,977,026	10.9	1,983,967	10.8	2,018,100	10.8
Almaty City	1,801,993	9.9	1,854,656	10.1	1,916,782	10.3
Karaganda	1,380,538	7.6	1,378,533	7.5	1,376,827	7.4
East Kazakhstan	1,383,745	7.6	1,378,527	7.5	1,369,635	7.4
Nur-Sultan City	1,030,577	5.7	1,078,384	5.9	1,136,008	6.1
Zhambyl	1,117,220	6.2	1,125,442	6.1	1,130,276	6.1
Shymkent City	952,170	5.2	1,009,086	5.5	1,036,144	5.6
Aktobe	857,711	4.7	869,637	4.7	881,728	4.7
Kostanay	875,616	4.8	872,795	4.7	868,524	4.7
Kyzylorda	783,156	4.3	794,334	4.3	803,545	4.3
Pavlodar	754,854	4.2	753,853	4.1	752,252	4.0
Akmola	738,942	4.1	738,587	4.0	736,682	4.0
Mangistau	660,317	3.6	678,199	3.7	698,919	3.8
West Kazakhstan	646,927	3.6	652,325	3.5	656,974	3.5
Atyrau	620,684	3.4	633,791	3.4	645,371	3.5
North Kazakhstan	558,584	3.1	554,517	3.0	548,751	2.9

Source: Government of Kazakhstan, Ministry of National Economy, Committee on Statistics.

Table A2.4: Urban and Rural Population

2019	Urban Population	Rural Population	Share of Urban Population (%)	Share of Rural Population (%)
Republic of Kazakhstan	10,893,810	7,738,359	58.5	41.5
Turkestan	405,536	1,612,564	20.1	79.9
Almaty region	451,568	1,604,083	22.0	78.0
Mangistau	276,705	422,214	39.6	60.4
Zhambyl	448,376	681,900	39.7	60.3
Kyzylorda	358,131	445,414	44.6	55.4
North Kazakhstan	252,821	295,930	46.1	53.9
Akmola	348,109	388,573	47.3	52.7
Atyrau	333,472	311,899	51.7	48.3
West Kazakhstan	344,497	312,477	52.4	47.6
Kostanay	478,916	389,608	55.1	44.9
East Kazakhstan	849,763	519,872	62.0	38.0
Pavlodar	530,980	221,272	70.6	29.4
Aktobe	628,067	253,661	71.2	28.8
Karaganda	1,097,935	278,892	79.7	20.3
Nur-Sultan City	1,136,008		100.0	0.0
Almaty City	1,916,782		100.0	0.0
Shymkent City	1,036,144		100.0	0.0

Source: Government of Kazakhstan, Ministry of National Economy, Committee on Statistics.

Table A2.5: Branch Network of Second-Tier Banks and Microfinance Organization Offices

No.	Region	Network of Branches and Outlets of Second-Tier Banks as of 3 May 2020			Number of Registered MFOs as of 1 Jan 2020
		Branches	Outlets	Total	
1	Astana / Nur-Sultan City	26	156	182	22
2	Akmola	16	57	73	1
3	Almaty City	22	314	336	82
4	Almaty region	16	86	102	7
5	Aktobe	17	81	98	3
6	Atyrau	18	66	84	3
7	East Kazakhstan	27	150	177	4
8	Zhambyl	14	54	68	3
9	West Kazakhstan	14	65	79	10

continued on next page

Table A2.5 *continued*

No.	Region	Network of Branches and Outlets of Second-Tier Banks as of 3 May 2020			Number of Registered MFOs as of 1 Jan 2020
		Branches	Outlets	Total	
10	Karaganda	25	155	180	16
11	Kyzylorda	12	41	53	11
12	Kostanay	13	76	89	7
13	Mangistau	19	75	94	3
14	Pavlodar	21	87	108	2
15	North Kazakhstan	14	45	59	3
16	Shymkent City	20	64	84	14
17	Turkestan	9	46	55	9
	Total	**303**	**1,618**	**1,921**	**200**

MFO = microfinance organization.

Source: National Bank of Kazakhstan.

Table A2.6: Mobile Phone Users, Ages 6 Years or Older
(%)

National Indicator	2015	2016	2017	2018
Total	**82.2**	**89.5**	**91.2**	**93.0**
Urban	84.0	91.5	92.7	94.1
Rural	80.0	86.9	89.1	91.3
Male	82.1	90.3	91.7	93.7
Female	82.4	88.8	90.7	92.3
Regions:				
Akmola	70.6	86.0	87.4	90.6
Aktobe	79.8	89.0	92.7	94.2
Almaty region	88.2	91.7	93.3	95.7
Atyrau	80.8	89.6	92.9	88.9
West Kazakhstan	88.9	93.1	92.1	92.6
Zhambyl	75.2	80.9	88.8	94.4
Karaganda	80.0	85.5	89.2	89.3
Kostanay	83.4	92.6	94.9	95.2
Kyzylorda	77.0	90.5	89.3	93.1
Mangistau	83.7	88.1	90.1	91.6
South Kazakhstan	81.1	90.5	92.6	...
Pavlodar	86.6	90.3	88.1	91.0
North Kazakhstan	81.1	84.4	88.1	89.3
Turkestan	...	...	...	92.9

continued on next page

Table A2.6 *continued*

National Indicator	2015	2016	2017	2018
East Kazakhstan	72.5	92.0	89.3	92.4
Nur–Sultan City	88.2	99.9	96.3	98.8
Almaty City	92.7	87.4	89.8	91.9
Shymkent City				94.0

Source: Government of Kazakhstan, Ministry of National Economy, Committee on Statistics.

Table A2.7: People with Access to the Internet
(%)

National Indicator	2015	2016	2017	2018
Total	**58.9**	**69.2**	**79.4**	**81.5**
Urban	67.1	66.1	66.0	66.4
Rural	32.9	33.9	34.0	33.6
Regions:				
Akmola	60.4	60.0	72.8	75.8
Aktobe	58.7	70.5	86.7	88.0
Almaty region	67.2	78.5	85.5	89.4
Atyrau	68.2	73.1	82.8	82.8
West Kazakhstan	86.5	92.1	96.7	95.0
Zhambyl	72.4	91.0	99.2	97.4
Karaganda	57.9	66.8	72.4	83.6
Kostanay	62.9	79.0	78.6	78.8
Kyzylorda	32.1	62.1	71.6	75.1
Mangistau	26.6	83.8	92.2	97.1
South Kazakhstan	81.2	86.0	95.6	...
Pavlodar	32.1	63.7	74.5	77.0
North Kazakhstan	51.5	64.0	73.7	74.8
Turkestan	...	...	...	98.9
East Kazakhstan	43.0	56.2	62.6	63.0
Nur–Sultan City	46.8	36.0	76.2	75.6
Almaty City	59.9	58.6	64.6	63.6
Shymkent City	...	...	...	98.5

Source: Government of Kazakhstan, Ministry of National Economy, Committee on Statistics.

APPENDIX 3

Microfinance Organizations Recommended for Participation in ADB's Sovereign Loan Program

Based on the analysis, the target client segment for ADB's sovereign loan program[1] should be micro and small enterprises in regions outside Almaty, principally in rural and remote areas.[2]

The 15 largest microfinance organizations (MFOs) in Kazakhstan have been considered for this assignment, as well as MFOs created with the participation of the National Chamber of Entrepreneurs of the Republic of Kazakhstan "Atameken" (NCE) which have been experiencing rapid growth. The MFOs' performance[3] was checked to determine whether they met the eligibility criteria (Table A3.1) as of 1 January 2020.

Table A3.1: Eligibility Criteria

Criteria	Standard
A. Compliant with NBK Prudential Ratios	Yes
1. k1 (equity to total assets ratio of at least 10%)	10% minimum
2. k2 (cap single borrower: 25% of equity)	25% maximum
3. k3 (liabilities <10x of equity)	10x maximum
B. Capital Adequacy (as per NBK regulation) of no less than the higher between	
1. 30% over NBK prudential requirement	15%
2. 15%	
C. Leverage Ratio not exceeding NBK limit less 30% (10x less 30% = 7x)	7x
D. Net PAR30 over Equity not exceeding 10%	<10%
E. Be profitable (basis is net profit after tax)	
F. Has audited financial statements prepared in accordance with the IFRS for the last 3 years	Based on IFRS

IFRS = International Financial Reporting Standards, NBK = National Bank of Kazakhstan, PAR = portfolio at risk.

Source: Asian Development Bank.

The MFOs' performance appeared to have been affected by the coronavirus disease (COVID-19) quarantine measures.

---

[1]   ADB's Sovereign Lending Program is partnering with the Damu Fund as the executor of the deal.
[2]   Based on statistics provided in the report. Table 8: Credit Activity of Small and Medium-Sized Enterprises; Figure 3: Active Micro, Small and Medium Enterprises in Regions, 2019; Table 21: Breakdown of Banks' Loan Portfolios by Region, 2019; Table 38: Loan Portfolio of Microfinance Organizations by Region.
[3]   The data available for analysis were used, including those obtained in the course of interviews. Much of the data are not public information, such as the portfolio at risk (PAR) indicator or the availability of audited financial statements.

For example, the portfolio at risk (PAR) indicator "PAR> 30 days + restructured" had grown to 4.6% at the end of Q1 2020 from 4.1% at the beginning of 2020 at Kazakhstan Loan Fund (KMF), and 3.3% from 2.6% at Arnur Credit. At the same time, "PAR> 30 days + restructured" did not include loan restructuring done in relation to government efforts to mitigate the impact of quarantine measures on customers' businesses. According to KMF and Arnur Credit, 60% of loan portfolios (on balance) have been restructured (changing payment schedules and prolonging loan maturities). According to MFOs, 80% of the restructured portfolio is expected to return to the normal while 20% will deteriorate.

Arnur Credit expects an increase in PAR> 30 days to at least 5% in 2020. However, there is uncertainty regarding the development of the situation in Kazakhstan and in global economies due to governments' COVID-19 measures, and these are only a preliminary estimate.

The MFOs under consideration were grouped into four categories based on the degree of compliance with the eligibility conditions for participation in the program, as well as possible funding amounts based on their business size and development plans. For the calculations (Table A3.2), the assumption was that there would be no significant deterioration in the economy of Kazakhstan, and MFOs would be able to keep the risk portfolio at the current level (with coefficient PAR30 less than 10%).

Group 1: MFOs are fully compliant and eligible to participate in the program. This group includes KMF, Arnur Credit, and Asian Credit Fund. The assessment of possible amounts of funding for MFOs are $23 million for KMF, $5 million for Arnur Credit, and $2 million for Asian Credit Fund (ACF).[4] Total funding is $30 million.

Group 2: MFOs that could participate in the program under certain conditions. These MFOs are mainly engaged in consumer or auto-lending, and the target small and medium-sized enterprise (SME) borrowers in their portfolios is up to 15%.

This group includes OnlineKazFinance, Shinhan Finance, and potentially, MFOs that were not interviewed: BNK Finance Kazakhstan and MK Finance. OnlineKazFinance[5] and Shinhan Finance meet regulatory eligibility criteria and could receive targeted financing for SME lending. The amount of funding is estimated at $2 million for each MFO.

Group 3: Small MFOs with growth potential: Bereke, GFM, and MiG Credit Astana with financing capacity of up to $2.7 million.

Group 4: Quasi-public sector MFOs with local authorities or NCE participation in the capital, which are working with SMEs in rural areas and regions. They provide loans at a subsidized/preferential rate for state programs and have the appropriate internal infrastructure. It is recommended to observe these MFOs' development. In the future, if they start working with commercial loans on market conditions, they may be good partners for the program as they have a target group of clients.

The amount of funding is conservatively estimated at $3.6 million. However, this group has a greater capacity for financing, given their growth potential.

---

[4]   Asian Credit Fund (ACF) did not demonstrate a desire to participate in the program, although we believe that negotiations can be continued with ACF.
[5]   Shinhan Finance has a capital adequacy threshold of 14%.

Table A3.2: Compliance with Eligibility Criteria

#	# by assets	Microfinance Organization	Assets	Granted Microcredits (net of reserves)	Liabilities	Equity	Income (uncovered loss)	Type	Region	(a) Compliant with NBK Prudential Ratios			(b) Capital Adequacy (as per NBK regulation) of no less than the higher between i) 30% over NBK prudential requirement; ii) 15% (>=15%)
										k1 (equity to total assets ratio of at least 10%)	k2 (cap single borrower: 25% of equity)	k3 (liabilities <10x of equity)	
		Total	355,217	293,336	246,609	108,608	23,260	Total					
1	1	KMF	147,592	132,770	111,078	36,514	12,822	Classical	Almaty	x	x	x	25%
2	2	Toyota Financial Services	69,121	56,042	61,003	8,118	1,932	Car loans	Almaty	x	x	x	12%
3	3	OnlineKazFinance	19,969	18,044	17,242	2,728	1,704	Online loans	Almaty	x	x	x	14%
4	4	Arnur Credit	19,925	16,422	14,677	5,248	1,266	Classical	Shymkent	x	x	x	26%
5	5	"Yrys" LLP	10,435	8,489	4,279	6,156	145	Quasi-state	Turkestan	x	x	x	59%
6	6	Asian Credit Fund	7,717	6,861	6,023	1,693	418	Classical	Almaty	x	x	x	22%
7	7	Shinhan Finance	7,632	7,354	1,900	5,731	432	Car loans	Almaty	x	x	x	75%
8	8	Regional investment center "Kyzylorda"	5,451	4,199	2,613	2,839	62	Quasi-state	Kyzylorda	x	x	x	52%
9	9	BNK Finance Kazakhstan	3,797	1,897	24	3,773	57	Car, consumer loans	Almaty	x	x	x	99%
10	10	MK-Finance	3,335	3,257	3,108	227	97	Car loans (Astana Motors)	Almaty	x	x	x	7%
11	11	ERG Microfinance	3,307	2,082	21	3,285	292	n/a	Nur-Sultan	x	x	x	99%
12	12	Bereke	3,040	2,268	2,067	973	67	Classical	Semey	x	x	x	32%
13	13	Finbox	3,032	528	167	2,865	1,549	n/a	Almaty	x	x	x	94%
14	14	GFM	2,657	2,483	386	2,272	51	Trade industry	Shymkent	x	x	x	86%
15	15	Central Asia "Microfinancial organization"	2,465	1,817	1,666	799	113	n/a	Almaty	x	x	x	32%
16	16	MiG Credit Astana	2,368	2,104	549	1,819	291	Construction industry	Nur-Sultan	x	x	x	77%
17	17	Taraz	2,279	261	2,004	275	0	Quasi-state	Taraz	x	x	x	12%
18	23	Atameken	1,384	1,263	759	625	22	Atameken	Aktau	x	x	x	45%
19	25	Atameken Taraz	1,131	962	498	634	17	Atameken	Taraz	x	x	x	56%
20	27	Atameken Kostanai	1,035	957	441	594	1	Atameken	Kostanai	x	x	x	57%
21	85	Atameken Qaragandy	161	55	66	95	-23	Atameken	Karagangy	x	x	x	59%
22	121	Atameken Atyrau	72	0	0	72	0	Atameken	Atyrau	x	x	x	100%

continued on next page

Estimated ADB funds ($ million)			
Group 1	Group 2	Group 3	Group 4
30.1	3.8	2.7	3.6

ADB = Asian Development Bank, FS = financial statements, IFRS = International Financial Reporting Standards, LP = loan portfolio, NBK = National Bank of Kazakhstan, PAR = portfolio at risk.

Source: Calculated using data from the National Bank of Kazakhstan (NBK).

Table A3.2 *continued*

#	(c) Leverage Ratio not exceeding NBK limit less 30% (<= 7x)	(d) Net PAR30 over Equity (not exceeding 10%)	Net PAR30, T million	(d) Yes or No	PAR30 at 01.01.2020	(e) Be profitable (basis is net profit after tax)	(f) Has audited FSs prepared accordance with IFRS (3 last years)	Coverage of the target group (remote regions, rural and micro borrowers)	% of LP growth assumption	Plans for growth/growth assumption (T million)	Funding needs assumption, mln $	ADB funds: assumption, mln $	ADB funds: assumption, T million
												40.3	
1	3	11.1%	4063	no	3.1%	yes	yes	66%	14%	18,588	45.9	22.9	9,294
2	8	4.1%	336	yes	0.6%	yes	yes	~15%	45%	25,219	62.3		
3	6	23.2%	632	no	3.5%	yes	yes	~15%	30%	5,413	13.4	2.0	812
4	3	9.0%	474	yes	3.3%	yes	yes	74%	25%	4,106	10.1	5.1	2,053
5	1	13.5%	832	no	9.8%	yes	n/a	61%	20%	1,698	4.2	2.1	849
6	4	11.8%	199	no	2.9%	yes	yes	93%	25%	1,715	4.2	2.1	858
7	0	0.9%	51	yes	0.7%	yes	yes	~15%	20%	1,471	3.6	1.8	735
8	1				n/a	yes	n/a	100%	20%	840	2.1	1.0	420
9	0				n/a	yes	n/a	n/a		0	0.0		
10	14				n/a	yes	n/a	low		0	0.0		
11	0				n/a	yes	n/a	n/a		0	0.0		
12	2	5.6%	54	yes	2.4%	yes	yes	71%	15%	340	0.8	0.4	170
13	0				n/a	yes	n/a	n/a		0	0.0		
14	0				n/a	yes	n/a	~high	40%	993	2.5	1.2	497
15	2				n/a	yes	n/a	n/a		0	0.0		
16	0	19.7%	358	no	up to 17%	yes	n/a	low	40%	842	2.1	1.0	421
17	7	0.0%	0	yes	0.0%	yes	n/a	high	30%	78	0.2	0.1	39
18	1	3.3%	21	yes	1.7%	yes	n/a	high	10%	126	0.3	0.2	63
19	0	0.0%	0	yes	0.0%	yes	n/a	high	10%	96	0.2	0.1	48
20	1	1.1%	7	yes	0.7%	yes	n/a	high	10%	96	0.2	0.1	48
21	1	0.0%	0	yes	0.0%	no	n/a	high	300%	165	0.41		
22	0	0.0%	0	yes	0.0%	yes	n/a	high	10%	0	0.0		

APPENDIX 4
Key Microfinance Organizations

This section contains non-public information which has been provided to ADB for internal use only.

The following information has been gathered from interviews with the MFOs' managers, corporate websites, and NBK data. It is not sufficient to assess large MFOs' business situations but can help assess the microfinance market.

Table A4.1: Microfinance Organization Ranking by Assets

Change in Ranking, 2017-2019	Microfinance Organization	Assets in T million			Growth, Y-o-Y		Total		
		2017	2018	2019	2018/ 2017	2019/ 2018	2017	2018	2019
1/1/1	KMF	96,807	129,229	147,592	33%	14%	51%	50%	42%
2/2/2	Toyota Financial Services	22,983	35,454	69,121	54%	95%	12%	14%	19%
22/7/3	OnlineKazFinance (Solva)	634	5,836	19,969	821%	242%	0%	2%	6%
4/3/4	Arnur Credit	8,542	14,771	19,925	73%	35%	5%	6%	6%
3/4/5	Yrys	10,622	10,289	10,435	(3%)	1%	6%	4%	3%
6/6/6	Asian Credit Fund	4,553	5,824	7,717	28%	33%	2%	2%	2%
7/7/7	Shinhan Finance	3,119	4,459	7,632	43%	71%	2%	2%	2%
15/9	BNK Finance	-	1,834	3,797	N/A	107%	0%	1%	1%
10	MK-Finance	-	-	3,335	N/A	N/A	0%	0%	1%
10/10/12	Bereke	2,018	2,952	3,040	46%	3%	1%	1%	1%
30/23/14	MFO GFM	420	814	2,657	94%	227%	0%	0%	1%
16/12/16	MiG Credit Astana	821	2,151	2,368	162%	10%	0%	1%	1%
24/17/13	Finbox	602	1,560	3,032	159%	94%	0%	1%	1%
19/19/23	MFO Atameken Mangistau	760	1,161	1,384	53%	19%	0%	0%	0%
23/21/25	MFO Atameken Taraz	609	893	1,131	47%	27%	0%	0%	0%
15/20/27	MFO Kostanay	868	1,115	1,035	28%	(7%)	0%	0%	0%
0/0/113	MFO Atameken Pavlodar	-	-	83	N/A	N/A	0%	0%	0%
	Total	188,462	256,516	355,217	36%	38%	100%	100%	100%

( ) = negative, KMF = Kazakhstan Loan Fund, MFO = microfinance organization, Y-o-Y = year-on-year.

Source: The size of the assets according to the National Bank of Kazakhstan.

Table A4.2: Change in Top Microfinance Organizations' Loan Portfolios

Change in Ranking, 2017-2019	Microfinance Organization	Loans in T million			Growth, Y-o-Y		Total		
		2017	2018	2019	2018/ 2017	2019/ 2018	2017	2018	2019
1/1/1	KMF	87,265	117,396	132,770	35%	13%	55%	50%	42%
2/2/2	Toyota Financial Services	18,773	30,609	56,042	63%	83%	12%	14%	19%
22/7/3	OnlineKazFinance (Solva)	547	5,706	18,044	944%	216%	0%	2%	6%
4/3/4	Arnur Credit	6,956	12,081	16,422	74%	36%	4%	6%	6%
3/4/5	Yrys	9,203	8,424	8,489	(8%)	1%	6%	4%	3%
6/6/6	Asian Credit Fund	3,989	5,130	6,861	29%	34%	2%	2%	2%
7/7/7	Shinhan Finance	2,672	4,422	7,354	66%	66%	2%	2%	2%
15/9	BNK Finance	–	182	1,897	N/A	945%	0%	1%	1%
10	MK-Finance	–	–	3,257	N/A	N/A	0%	0%	1%
10/10/12	Bereke	1,616	2,028	2,268	25%	12%	1%	1%	1%
30/23/14	MFO GFM	313	606	2,483	94%	310%	0%	0%	1%
16/12/16	MiG Credit Astana	596	1,373	2,104	130%	53%	0%	1%	1%
24/17/13	Finbox	457	651	528	42%	(19%)	0%	1%	1%
19/19/23	MFO Atameken Mangistau	724	1,078	1,263	49%	17%	0%	0%	0%
23/21/25	MFO Atameken Taraz	465	582	962	25%	65%	0%	0%	0%
15/20/27	MFO Kostanay	693	909	957	31%	5%	0%	0%	0%
0/0/113	MFO Atameken Pavlodar	–	–	16	N/A	N/A	0%	0%	0%
	Total	159,956	219,454	293,336	37%	34%	100%	100%	100%

( ) = negative, KMF = Kazakhstan Loan Fund, MFO = microfinance organization, Y-o-Y = year-on-year.

Source: The size of the assets according to the National Bank of Kazakhstan.

Kazakhstan Loan Fund

The Kazakhstan Loan Fund (KMF) is a leader in the microfinance sector in both Kazakhstan and Central Asia. It has been operating for more than 20 years, with around 2,000 employees and 110 sales points through 14 branches and 7 sub-offices in more than 4,000 locations in major cities of Kazakhstan.

At the end of 2019, the company had assets worth $387.2 million and a capital of $129.4 million. It has attracted 92% of funds in foreign currency and 8% in local currency (ADB: T3 billion, Altyn Bank: T5.2 billion).

The company plans to have increased its loan portfolio by 10.8% in 2020. With loans to SMEs accounting for 8% of the total loan portfolio, the company plans to raise it to 15%.

The company stands for high-quality portfolio growth and limits its clients' borrowing capacity: no more than two simultaneous loans in other banks are allowed for new clients, and no more than three for active clients. Most of KMF's clients do have loans from other lending institutions and banks (67%)—consumer lending by Halyk Bank, Kaspi Bank, and Eurasian Bank, as well as commodity loans at marketplaces play a significant role in this regard.

The KMF management noted a decrease in consumer demand for loans: the terms and amounts of loans are growing in the market, with a long-term impact of 2015 devaluation.

The social impact of KMF's operations shows that 67% of its clients, i.e., 166,000 people, are rural residents. More than 143,000 women received KMF loans, accounting for 58% of all MFO clients.

Table A4.3: Kazakhstan Loan Fund Performance Indicators

Item	2017	2018	2019
$:T exchange rate	332.33	384.2	382.59
Gross loan portfolio (T million)	87,584.2	118,463.3	134,880.1
Loan portfolio growth (%)	70.1	35.3	13.9
Number of active clients	220,903	243,715	248,007
Growth in number of active clients	20.5%	10.3%	1.8%
Number of female clients	62%	60%	58%
Clients from rural areas	66%	67%	67%
Average outstanding loan (T million)	0.396	0.486	0.544
PAR>30 days + restructured (%)	2.4	2.0	4.1
Number of employees	1,693	1,908	1,960
Number of credit employees (%)	49	55	52

PAR = portfolio at risk.

Source: Kazakhstan Loan Fund.

At the end of 2018, KMF's net profit amounted to T10 billion. KMF profitability indicators in 2018 totaled 8.9% for return on assets (RoA) and 41.2% for return on equity (RoE). The company offers loan products designed for the population's needs and aimed at supporting entrepreneurship as well as the development of agriculture.

Table A4.4: Credit Products for All Client Segments

Item	Group Loan Dostar	Individual Loan Shanyrak
Objectives	1) for business development 2) for economy development 3) for consumption purposes	for housing improvement (construction works)
Amount	up to T5 million, step-by-step structure	up to T3 million, up to T1 million for new customers, up to T2 million for repeat clients
Term	3–60 months 3–36 months for entrepreneurs	3–60 months
Collateral	Group joint and several liability for clients group uniting from 2 to 10 people	without collateral for individuals
Repayment source	1) entrepreneurial activity; 2) wages; 3) agricultural / farming activities	
Repayment	annuity or in equal installments	
Lead time	starting from 1 day	up to 3 days

Source: Kazakhstan Loan Fund corporate website (https://kmf.kz/).

Table A4.5: Loan Products for Individuals

Item	KMF Fast Turbo	KMF Fast	Standard
Objectives	for Consumption Purposes		
Amount	from T5,000 to T125,000	From T125,001 to T1 million	up to T10 million, up to T1 million for new customers, up to T2 million for repeat customers
Term	Up to 45 days	3–36 months	3–60 months
Collateral	without collateral		
Repayment source	wage		
Repayment	annuity or in equal installments		
Lead time	online loan within 15 minutes	starting from 1 day	

Source: Kazakhstan Loan Fund (KMF) corporate website (https://kmf.kz/).

Table A4.6: Loan Products for Entrepreneurs and Farmers

Item	Microenterprises	SME / SME Agro
Objectives	1) for business development 2) for economy development	
Amount	from T50,000 to T10 million	from T10 million to T20 million
Term	3–36 months for farmers: 3–60 months	3–60 months

continued on next page

Table A4.6 *continued*

Item	Microenterprises	SME / SME Agro
Collateral	Required	Required
Repayment source	1) operating business 2) agricultural/farming activities	1) operating business 2) agricultural/farming activities
Repayment	annuity or in equal installments	
	for farmers: with a grace period for repayment of the principal amount of debt up to 11 months in each year	
Lead time	Starting from 1 day	

SMEs = small and medium-sized enterprises.

Source: Kazakhstan Loan Fund corporate website (https://kmf.kz/).

KMF planned to launch in February 2020 online loans of T125,000 with a term of up to 45 days. Since 2013, KMF, with the support of the KMF-Demeu Fund, has been implementing the Project for Increasing Financial Literacy of Population of the Republic of Kazakhstan. By 1 January 2019, the number of participants in the project exceeded 137,000 people.

KMF's training needs have been identified as MFO strategic marketing; innovation in financial analysis, MFO sales management, talent management and talent pool creation, calculation of the annual interest rate, and debt burden ratios in accordance with the new legislation.

Toyota Financial Services

Toyota Financial Services (TFS) began its operation in Kazakhstan in 2014. The Kazakhstani MFO was established by Toyota Financial Services UK, owned by Toyota Financial Services Corporation (Japan), which belongs to Toyota Motor Corporation.

Of the company's clients, 90% are individuals. In 2018, the MFO began working with legal entities. The average amount of a car loan is about T9 million. As a part of the MFO lending limit, the maximum loan amount was T20 million per borrower, and T50 million from 1 January 2020. In addition to standard loans, clients are also offered leasing options which are used by larger enterprises.

TFS 2019 Performance Results
- Loan portfolio: T55.4 billion.
- TFS share of total Toyota sales in Kazakhstan for 11 months of 2019: 35.3%.
- For 11 months of 2019, TFS issued 6,251 loans (compared to 3,671 in 2018) worth more than T55 billion (T30.8 billion in 2018).

Figure A4.1: Toyota Financial Services' Loan Portfolio Growth

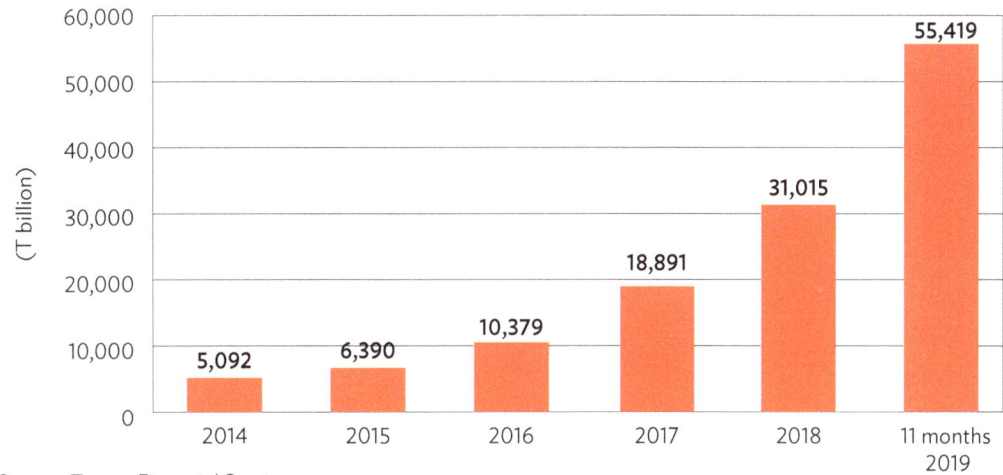

(T billion)

- 2014: 5,092
- 2015: 6,390
- 2016: 10,379
- 2017: 18,891
- 2018: 31,015
- 11 months 2019: 55,419

Source: Toyota Financial Services.

TFS demonstrates a good quality loan portfolio: the level of nonperforming loans (NPLs) is lower than the industry average, which amounted to 0.59% in 2019.

Figure A4.2: Nonperforming Loans 90+ Dynamics

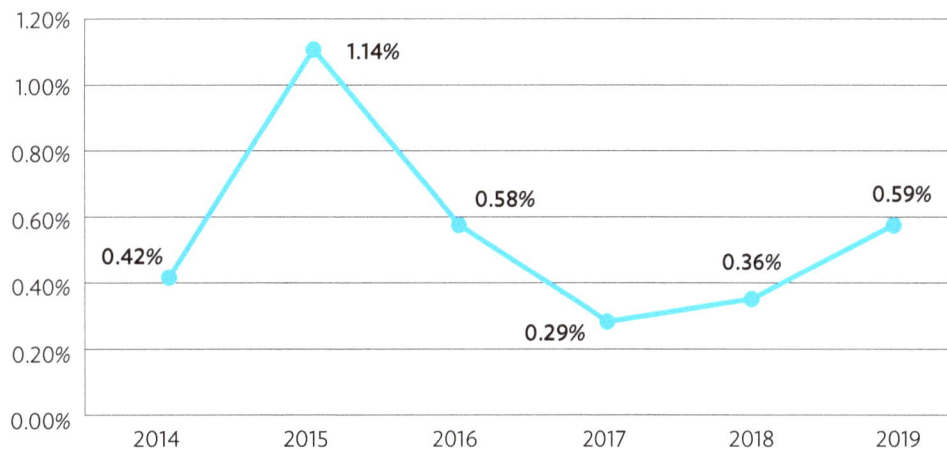

- 2014: 0.42%
- 2015: 1.14%
- 2016: 0.58%
- 2017: 0.29%
- 2018: 0.36%
- 2019: 0.59%

Source: Report provided by Toyota Financial Services.

Borrowers' creditworthiness scoring, application auto-approval, and verification are assessed in loan applications.

TFS has an extensive funding base, works with 12 Kazakhstan banks and the Damu Entrepreneurship Fund JSC (Damu Fund), and is interested in attracting direct financing from development institutions under the guarantees of Japanese financial institutions with high credit ratings.

TFS carries out trainings for its personnel, including trainings on risk analysis and assessment of clients' financial situations.

TFS has ambitious sales plans for 2020: to issue 6,263 loans totaling T57.8 billion.

Figure A4.3: Toyota Financial Services 2020 Sales Plan

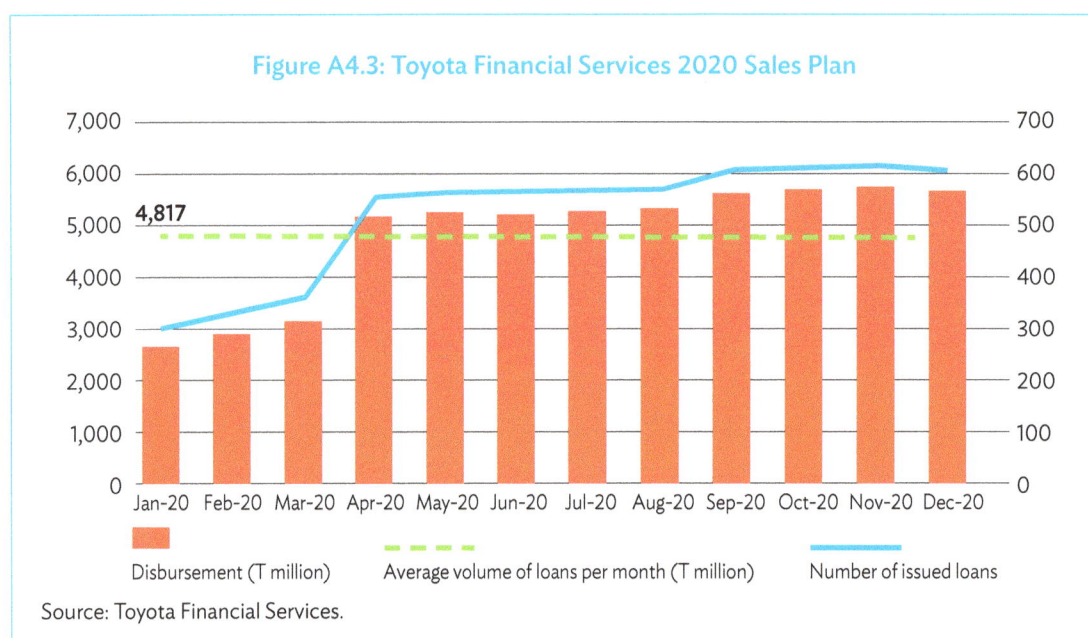

Disbursement (T million)   Average volume of loans per month (T million)   Number of issued loans

Source: Toyota Financial Services.

OnlineKazFinance

Solva is part of ID Finance's international financial group which operates in eight countries, including in Europe and Latin America, serving more than 3.5 million people. Among its clients, 85% regularly use its services.

The company started in 2012 in the Russian Federation with the Money Man brand (consumer loans to paychecks) and began in Kazakhstan in 2014. OnlineKazFinance was registered in 2016, and the Solva brand was created in 2017 to take the best practices and experience of its predecessors.

The company uses a unique scoring system created by Belarusian developers.

In Kazakhstan, OnlineKazFinance LLP has its head office in Almaty, along with a network of online and offline agencies with 74 points of contact with customers. In the spring of 2018, it became possible for clients to sign agreements through an electronic digital signature and in 2019, 30% of OnlineKazFinance clients used this option. Using SMS for signing (with one-time PIN technology) has been an option since 2020.

In the first quarter of 2019, MFOs began working with a new client segment: small businesses, self-employed, and the informal sector, providing loans of up to T2 million. By the end of 2019, this segment accounted for 15% of the MFO's loan portfolio.

OnlineKazFinance management noted that 30% of its clients are from Almaty and 70% are from other regions. The company planned to test factoring as a new product in 2020.

OnlineKazFinance issues two types of loans: payday loans with up to 45 days' maturity (Money Man) and standard loans with up to 18 months' maturity. These have an average interest rate of up to 38% per annum, with the cost of products pegged at about 30%.

NPLs (PAR90+) do not exceed 3.5%, according to OnlineKazFinance's management. The company's operating expenses, at 7–8%, are lower compared to the market average, as provided by the business model used.

OnlineKazFinance planned to issue bonds in the middle and end of 2020.

The company's management noted that the main credit barriers in the regions are the customers' lack of communication, access to the internet, open bank/card account, and electronic signature. Financially competent and knowledgeable customers want the best services that meet their needs.

Arnur Credit

Arnur Credit LLP is one of the leaders in the microfinance sector of Kazakhstan, operating in the south of the country. The organization's primary activity is issuing microloans to entrepreneurs, with a focus on supporting rural entrepreneurs in remote areas that do not have access to financial services.

Arnur Credit LLP was founded in 2001. The company's head office is in Shymkent, and it has 9 branches and 43 offices, including 33 offices in rural areas. The major operation is concentrated in the Turkestan region and Shymkent.

Table A4.7: Loan Portfolio by Region, 31 December 2019

Region	Loan Portfolio Outstanding (T million)	Share in Gross Loan Portfolio (%)
Turkestan	10,121	59.6%
Shymkent City	3,531	20.8%
Kyzylorda	1,512	8.9%
Jambyl	1,004	5.9%
Almaty	610	3.6%
Almaty City	211	1.2%
Total	**16,988**	**100.0%**

Source: Arnur Credit.

Arnur Credit's loan portfolio demonstrated rapid growth in 2017–2018, followed by a relative slowdown in 2019. Arnur Credit's management plans to increase the loan portfolio by 40% in 2020 and 30% in 2021. However, these plans will be adjusted with another economic crisis in view.

Compared to the figures at the start of 2019, the number of active clients has decreased due to these reasons:

1. The government repaid microloans to 2,279 clients, following the president's decree to provide timely aid to decrease the population's over-indebtedness.

2. Due to the growth of PAR in consumer behavior scoring, the disbursements on this product were suspended in the Almaty branch and the disbursements of unsecured microloans were limited in the Taraz branch, meaning the approval of the loans was made at the risk management department level.

3. The seasonality of agriculture microcredits influenced the number of clients, with the smaller loans for agriculture purposes repaid in the fourth quarter of 2019.

Table A4.8: Arnur Credit Performance Indicators

Item	2017	2018	2019
$:T exchange rate	332.33	384.2	382.59
Gross loan portfolio (T million)	7,539	12,608	16,988
Loan portfolio growth (%)	74	67.2	34.7
Number of active clients	13,014	22,557	19,704
Growth in number of active clients (%)	39	73	-13
Female clients (%)	45	n/a	36
Clients from rural areas (%)	74	n/a	74
Average outstanding loan (T million)	0.579	0.492	0.862
PAR>30 days (%)	1.4	1.3	1.7
Number of employees	164	218	258
Credit employees (%)	60	58	60
RoA (%)	7.8	7.3	7.3
RoE (%)	18.4	21.0	26.8
Cost of funds (%)	17.7	18.8	19.1
Portfolio yield (%)	33.2	35.0	34.7

PAR = portfolio at risk, RoA = return on assets, RoE = return on equity,

Source: Arnur Credit.

Arnur Credit specializes in issuing business loans: agriculture loans made up 49% of its loan portfolio; entrepreneurial non-agriculture loans, 41%; and consumer loans, 10%. The average loan amount has grown by 49% over the past 2 years.

Table A4.9: Arnur Credit Loan Portfolio Structure

Loan Purpose	Outstanding Portfolio		Active Loans	
	Outstanding loans (T million)	Share, (%)	Number	Share, (%)
Agricultural	8,272	49	11,141	47
Entrepreneurial	7,014	41	4,990	21
Consumer	1,702	10	7,475	32
Total	**16,988**	**100**	**23,606**	**100**

Source: Arnur Credit.

Over the past years, Arnur Credit's loan portfolio maintained a good quality, with the amount of write-offs not exceeding 1.5% annually. The consumer loan portfolio has a higher risk (PAR> 30 increased to 3.86%) compared to the rest of the portfolio.

Table A4.10: Arnur Credit Portfolio Quality by Loan Products

Loans (T million)	2017		2018		2019	
	Portfolio	PAR>30 (%)	Portfolio	PAR>30 (%)	Portfolio	PAR>30 (%)
Rural loans	3,697	1.13	5,844	1.04	8,275	1.47
Entrepreneurial loans	2,835	1.40	4,870	1.14	7,017	1.56
Consumer loans	1,007	2.39	1,894	2.43	1,696	3.86
Total	**7,539**	**1.40**	**12,608**	**1.29**	**16,988**	**1.74**

Source: Arnur Credit.

The total amount of unsecured loans as of 31 December 2019 was T 4.92 billion (28.9% from gross loan portfolio). The following branches have the highest portion of unsecured loans in its portfolio: Kyzylorda (60.3%), Yassy (45.8%), Taraz (42.5%), and Keles (41.5%).

The technical assistance from the European Bank for Reconstruction and Development (EBRD) in the Women in Business and SME Institutional Development Capacity Building programs continued in 2020. Within the framework of the Bikesh project under the Women in Business program, the trainings and seminars (*Syrlasy*) for active and potential clients, specifically businesswomen, continued. Within the framework of the EBRD program, the trainings on financial analysis and putting credit opinion together will be conducted for loan officers.

For Arnur Credit's training needs, the management plans to update the strategic plan and attract external consultants for strategic sessions.

In 2019, there was a significant expansion of the lenders' network, including the signed agreement with large strategical partners International Finance Corporation (IFC) (the loan agreement with IFC for $4 million was signed) and ADB (T1 billion was received from the Damu Fund). In the beginning of

2019, the second tranche for $1 million was received from EBRD within the framework of Arnur Credit SME financing, as well as financing of women entrepreneurs for $1 million.

Arnur Credit attracted funding worth T7.3 billion in 2019, all of which was in the national currency, avoiding foreign exchange risks.

A $4-million loan from IFC and T900 million from the Damu Fund are expected to have been received in the first quarter of 2020.

Yrys

Yrys is a subsidiary of LLP RIC ONTUSTIK and LLP Center for Entrepreneurship Services. Yrys has been operating in the lending market since April 2009, with its head office in Turkestan.

The priority areas of financing for Yrys include support for agriculture projects, as well as socially significant projects such as the creation of feedlots and market-milk dairies, development and creation of greenhouse farms, crop processing, and production of consumer goods and the provision of services.

Yrys finances individual entrepreneurs, peasant/farm enterprises, and legal entities in the Turkestan region. It offers the following types of microloan financing:

- from own funds: interest rate not exceeding 7% per annum, financing term up to 5 years;
- from attracted funds: interest rate not exceeding 14% per annum, financing term up to 5 years; and
- financial leasing: interest rate not exceeding 9% per annum, financing term up to 5 years.

Loans from own funds were placed at a rate of 17% on a short-term basis.

The types of microcredit products are:

- Yrys-agro for crop production, greenhouse development, gardening;
- Yrys-livestock for livestock (fattening and herd expansion);
- Yrys-preferential for small and medium-sized businesses (priority projects);
- Yrys-business in rural areas for small and medium-sized businesses;
- Yrys-business for small and medium-sized businesses;
- Business Roadmap 2020 Program for SME participants in the program; and
- Yrys-leasing for small and medium-sized businesses.

Yrys applies a loyal collateral policy, accepting property not accepted by banks, such as adobe houses, sheep houses, and some types of land.

The funds were received from the Agrarian Credit Corporation (ACC) and the Damu Fund. In 2019, T950 million was received from the Damu Fund.

In each district and in the city of Turkestan, regional managers work to consult on loan conditions and the documents required for lending.

Table A4.11: Yrys Performance Indicators

Item	2017	2018	2019
$:T exchange rate	332.33	384.2	382.59
Gross loan portfolio (T million)	9,325.0	8,659.1	8,785.5
Loan portfolio growth (%)		(7.1)	1.5
Number of active clients	4,676	3,399	3,030
Growth in number of active clients (%)		(27.3)	(10.9)
Female clients	n/a	n/a	n/a
Clients from rural areas (%)	69.4	63.5	61.3
Average outstanding loan (T million)	2.0	2.5	2.9
PAR>30 days + restructured (%)	12.1	10.4	9.8
Number of employees	74	74	62
Credit employees (%)	35.1	41.9	35.5

PAR = portfolio at risk, ( ) = negative.

Source: Yrys.

More than 60% of Yrys clients live in rural areas. A grace period of 3–12 months is generally applied although in some cases, this could extend to 2 years. The average loan amount over the past 3 years has increased from T2 million to T2.9 million.

Yrys management noted that they did not see any problems with fund allocation, as there is a demand for their services from the market.

Until 2019, the Yrys head office was in Shymkent. After the transfer of the regional center, it moved its head office to Turkestan. According to the Yrys management, there are fewer qualified loan officers in Turkestan, so there is a need to train employees in credit and financial analysis, as well as in accounting standards.

Asian Credit Fund

Established in 1997 by international relief and development organization Mercy Corps as a micro and small-sized enterprise lending program, the Asian Credit Fund (ACF) provides financial services that are designed to promote the development of rural households and the growth of small businesses and home ownership throughout Kazakhstan. At the end of 2019, 75% of ACF's clients were women, and group loans made up 42% of its portfolio.

Table A4.12: Asian Credit Fund Performance Indicators

Item	2017	2018	2019
Number of offices	37	43	51
Gross loan portfolio (T million)	4,000	5,100	7,100
Loan portfolio growth (%)	39	28	39,2
Number of active clients	20,620	24,389	29,723
Growth in number of active clients (%)		18	22
Female clients (%)	n/a	n/a	75
Clients from rural areas (%)	n/a	n/a	93.0
Average outstanding loan (T million)	0.194	0.209	0.239
Par>30 days (%)	0.5	1.6	2.9
Number of employees	226	256	340
Number of credit employees (%)	51	45	49
RoA (%)	7.0	6.1	6.2
RoE (%)	34	28	28

PAR = portfolio at risk, RoA = return on assets, RoE = return on equity, ( ) = negative.

Source: Asian Credit Fund website (https://asiancreditfund.com/en/).

ACF's areas of operation are divided internally into three departments (Almaty, Saryagash, and Taldykorgan) and four branches (Karaganda, Semey, Shymkent, and Taraz).[6] The largest of these, according to loan size in the loan portfolio, are Almaty, Saryagash, and Taraz.

The average amount of ACF loans issued is one of the smallest in the MFO market, with the average loan balance at $622. A large number of small loans and clients' regional remoteness entail high operating costs (20%), with the average rate interest rate on loans at 42%.

ACF portfolio structure: one-third each in trade, livestock, and consumer loans.

Table A4.13: Asian Credit Fund Loan Products

Item	Group Credit (groups of 3 to 20 people)	Individual Loan	Individual Loan	Residential Energy Efficiency Loan (REEL)
Objective	to support and develop households engaged in trade, services and agriculture, wage earners	to finance working capital, purchase of equipment, livestock and for consumer purposes	to develop and expand business, repair commercial and residential real estate, for agricultural support and consumer purposes	For people living in rural regions for repair and construction works in their homes with energy efficiency improvement elements

continued on next page

6   Each department and branch has multiple offices that act as points of service.

Table A4.13 *continued*

Item	Group Credit (groups of 3 to 20 people)	Individual Loan	Individual Loan	Residential Energy Efficiency Loan (REEL)
Collateral	Unsecured, group solidarity	Unsecured	Required	Required
Loan amount, (T'000)	from 30 to 1,000 per group member	from 100 to 1,500	from 1,500 to 53,000	from 100 to 1,500
Loan term (months)	6–24	6–24	6–60	6–24
Annual effective interest rate (%)	from 49.8	from 49.8	from 48.37	from 49.8
Nominal interest rate (%)	from 41	from 41	from 32	from 41

Source: Asian Credit Fund website (https://asiancreditfund.com/en/).

At the end of 2019, ACF had 14 creditors (mainly foreign investment funds), including a loan from KazAgro in tenge at 14.5%. The borrowed funds' average cost at the end of 2019 was about 15% per annum.

ACF's personnel training needs concern new product development, models for quick customer assessment, master's degree in business admistration or MBA for branch managers, and team building. Training needs for ACF clients include launching a business and developing ideas for business.

Shinhan Finance

Shinhan Finance LLP is a large subsidiary of Shinhan Financial Group (Republic of Korea), with branches in the United States, the United Kingdom, Japan, the People's Republic of China, and India. In Kazakhstan, JSC Shinhan Bank Kazakhstan has operated since 2008 as a subsidiary of JSC Shinhan Bank (Seoul, Republic of Korea), which is also part of the structure of this corporation.

In Kazakhstan, Shinhan Finance started operating in 2017 and showed aggressive growth. It has offices in Almaty and Turkestan, and planned to open an office in Shymkent in 2020. Shinhan Finance specializes in issuing car loans, with 15–17% of loans issued for business purposes, and has a PAR>90 + 0.7%.

The group's internal resources are used for staff training, with external seminars organized for trainings in financial and tax accounting. All the trainings are accompanied by testing to check the knowledge level.

BNK Finance Kazakhstan

BNK Finance Kazakhstan provides consumer and car loans. The company's sole shareholder is BNK Capital from the Republic of Korea.[7] Established in March 2011, BNK Capital had $124.2 billion

---

[7]   Data from the BNK Finance Kazakhstan corporate site.

in assets by 2014. It has a staff of 8,282 people and an income of $177 million. BNK Capital has a network in emerging countries in Southeast Asia, advancing into the small-loan market in Cambodia, the Lao People's Democratic Republic, and Myanmar in 2014. It is enhancing the Republic of Korea's position as a loan-specializing financial company.

MC-Finance

MC-Finance was formed as a part of KMK Astana-Motors, a group of various car brands dealers, and was registered on 15 February 2019.[8] It offers lending programs for new car purchases from leading automobile brands represented in Astana Motors car dealerships, with a maximum amount of T20 million and terms of up to 7 years.

Table A4.14: MC-Finance Credit Products

No.	Product	Maximum Amount (T million)	Annual Rate (%)	Maximum Term	Collateral	Repayment
1	Classic program	20	19	7 years	Car purchased; down payment: 20% of the car cost.	Principal debt and interest: monthly
2	Easy program	20	n/a	3 years	Car purchased; minimum down payment: 35% of the car cost.	Interest rate: monthly; Principal debt: at the end of the term, or by selling a car to the Astana Motors car dealership
3	Loan for used cars sold through Astana Motors car dealership network	20	20	5 years	Car purchased; minimum down payment – 30% of the car cost.	of principal debt and interest – on a monthly basis.
4	For Subaru car	20	0,1	up to 1 year		
5	Soft loan program	20	from 9%	13–84 months		

Source: MC-Finance.

Bereke

Bereke was established in 2003 and provides microloans to the self-employed, entrepreneurs, and small businesses. The organization's head office is located in Semey. It has three branches in Ust-Kamenogorsk, Pavlodar, and Karaganda, and 19 sub-offices in Ayagoz, Urjar, Karauyl, Beskaragai, Aksu,

---

8   Data from the MC-Finance corporate site. https://mc-finance.kz.

Ekibastuz, Terenkol, Irtyshsk, Maysk, Zhelezinka, Zaysan, Zyryanovsk, Zharma, Kokpekty, Tarbagatay, Kurchum, Katon-Karagay, Karkaralynsk, and Temirtau.

Over the past 3 years, Bereke's loan portfolio growth has been declining. The company's management said the reasons for the decline include competition from the banking sector (card limits, consumer loans, installment goods, Kaspi Bank online loans), especially in urban areas.

Table A4.15: Bereke Performance Indicators

Item	2017	2018	2019
Loan portfolio net (T million)	1,616	2,028	2,268
Loan portfolio growth (%)	41	25	12
RoA (%)	4.4	4.5	2.2
RoE (%)	8.3	11.7	6.7
PAR>90 days, %	n/a	1.0	2.4
Number of active clients	n/a	n/a	4,539
Female clients	n/a	n/a	73
Clients from rural areas (%)	n/a	n/a	71
Average outstanding loan (T million)	n/a	n/a	0.503

PAR = portfolio at risk, RoA = return on assets, RoE = return on equity.

Source: Bereke, National Bank of Kazakhstan.

Bereke uses a conservative approach in credit risk assessment, allowing it to maintain a low PAR>90 (2.4%). It targeted a 15% portfolio growth in 2020, with inflation expected to provide significant contribution to the growth.

Bereke's key clients are individuals with private subsidiary farming. Clients who have a small business and are registered as an individual entrepreneur prefer to be treated as individuals when getting a loan.

Table A4.16: Bereke Credit Products

Product	Amount (T million)	Rate	Term (months)	Collateral
Individual	up to 8	n/a	up to 36	Inventory, motor transport, real estate, agricultural machinery, third party guarantee
Individual unsecured	up to 0.5	n/a	up to 12	Not required
Group	up to 1 (per group member)	n/a	up to 9	joint liability of two and more group members

Source: Bereke website (https://bereke.kz).

Interest rate on the microloans depends on the loan product and is established, as provided by the LLP internal credit policy. In 2019, rates varied: 36%–40% for business loans and 48% for consumer loans. The average lending rate in 2019 was 44%, with 42% planned for 2020. The company's operating expenses is rather high due to the regional offices' remoteness, accounting for 20%–22% of total expenditure.

Most loans are issued under a joint guarantee of the members of the lending group (76%).

Table A4.17: Bereke Loan Portfolio Structure by Type of Collateral

Loan Type	2018		2019	
	T million	%	T million	%
Loans secured by real estate	121	6	193	8
Loans secured by movable property	511	25	354	15
Unsecured loans (group guarantee)	1,409	69	1,736	76
Total	**2,042**	**100**	**2,283**	**100**

Source: Bereke financial statement (audited).

Bereke uses a system of limits for credit approval process and underwriting, which allows quick consideration of loan applications.

Bereke carried out trainings for personnel on evaluating the client's businesses, according to the Damu programs (analysis of agricultural projects), Microfinance Centre (general), and online learning EBRD program (training for branch directors). The chief executive officer noted the need for training for middle management, as well as sales and psychological training (building relationships, conflicts, and stresses management).

Table A3.18 shows the borrowed funds structure:

Table A4.18: Bereke Lenders

Lenders	2019	
agRIF Coöperatief U.A.	186	12%
ALTERFIN CVBA	179	12%
MIKRO KAPITAL S.a.r.l.	71	5%
responsAbility SICAV Lux SICAV (Lux) Micro and SMF Finance Debt Fund	77	5%
Grameen Credit Agricole Microfinance Foundation	238	16%
responsAbility Global Microfinance Funds	182	12%
responsAbility SICAV (LUX)	236	16%
Investing for Development SICAV- Luxembourg Micro	320	22%
Total	**1,488**	**100%**

Source: Bereke financial statement (audited).

Loans from investment funds were received under conditions that do not require collateral. All the loans have been received in tenge to expand the loan portfolio (creditors control the targeted use of borrowed funds). Bereke provides monthly, quarterly, and annual reports on how the borrowed funds have been used.

Bereke could not attract financing from the Damu Fund due to the requirements on collaterals, monitoring of borrowers, and small amounts of financing. Bereke believes the fund has a very low risk appetite compared to other lenders. According to Bereke managers, the borrowed resources have risen in price over the last period, and foreign investment funds offer financing without collateral at 18%–19% per annum in local currency.

GoldFinMarket

GoldFinMarket (GFM) was established in Taldykurgan in 2003 and moved to Shymkent in 2006. Its main activity is issuing microloans for the development of businesses in the Turkestan region. GFM issues group loans, SME loans, and retail loans. It is also working to develop a new product for feedlot for livestock in cooperation with the ACC.

According to information provided by GFM management, the average loan term is up to 1 year while the average loan amount is T1 million. NPL is held at 3%. GFM's loan portfolio is growing at about 100% per year, with monthly growth totaling T100 million There was potential to attract T2 billion in funding in 2020.

The information technology product technical development requires funds and resources. The company's management knows the market well and feels confident in the development of new products.

 GFM does not pursue financing from the Damu Fund as it does not consider the Damu Fund's conditions attractive: long application process, low appraisal of collateral, stringent monitoring conditions for end borrowers, and a mandatory limited rate for the end borrower that results in insufficient margin for MFOs.

GFM management noted a market trend in the flow of SME loans leaking into the retail segment.

MiG Credit Astana

MiG Credit Astana has been successfully operating since August 2010, with one office in Nur-Sultan and another office in Almaty.

At the end of 2019, the MiG Credit Astana's portfolio included about 500 clients. Business loans account for 85% of the portfolio (loan amounts of T100 million to T200 million); consumer loans for 5% (up to T15 million); and other loans for 10%. The main borrowers are SMEs in the construction sector (up to 60% of business loans). There are no agriculture loans offered. MiG Credit Astana issues loans to several borrowers under one collateral object, e.g., expensive real estate.

At the end of 2019, PAR>60 amounted to 17%. MiG Credit Astana management explained that such a high index by the construction business accounts for temporary delays. Loan write-offs for the balance sheet were minimal.

MiG Credit Astana has fine-tuned the process of issuing loans, with a review of the clients' business peculiarities and registration of collateral taking 1–3 days.

MiG Credit Astana had planned to launch online lending based on its scoring system, but the project was suspended after legislation restricted interest rates, making the project unattractive in terms of profitability.

MiG Credit Astana had previously funded lending activities from the founders' funds but as the business grew, there was a need to attract funds from other sources. In 2020, MiG Credit Astana's managers were aiming to attract financing worth T700 million.

Finbox

Finbox began operations in 2014 and has gained the trust of more than 91,000 clients in a short time. The company has an extensive regional network of 84 offices operating daily in 32 cities in Kazakhstan.[9] In 2017, the Finbox LLP rebranded and began to use the Akshamat trademark (without re-registering the MFO Finbox LLP).

The online service Finbox was created to issue urgent loans to the population in 15 minutes, using only a passport as a form of identification. An automated system makes the loan decision. To be approved for a loan, borrowers must be 21–60 years old and a citizen of Kazakhstan, and must have a stable source of income and a signature in a loan agreement in one of the company's branches. Loans are transferred to a bank card account or to a client's bank account. Repayment of loans is made in cash, through a terminal or online payment in Qiwi electronic payment system, or at the cash desk of an MFO branch.

The client has the right to repay the loan in annuity or differentiated payments, as well as at the end of the loan term.

Microfinance Organizations created by the National Chamber of Entrepreneurs of the Republic of Kazakhstan "Atameken" and local authorities

Since 2016, MFOs have been established with local executive authorities in the Mangistau, Zhambyl, and Kostanai regions.[10] In 2019, MFOs were also created in the Pavlodar and Karaganda regions.

From 2016 to 2019, RIC Kyzylorda LLP was operated in trust (it has been working independently since the contract expired). In February 2020, the National Chamber of Entrepreneurs of the Republic of

---

[9]   Data from the Finbox corporate website.
[10]   Data from the National Chamber of Entrepreneurs of the Republic of Kazakhstan "Atameken."

Kazakhstan "Atameken" (NCE) and *akimat* of Almaty created MFOs to cater to microbusinesses with an authorized capital of T300 million.

The NCE contributed 51% and the local executive bodies contributed 49% of funding to set up these MFOs. These MFOs operate under the Bastau and Yenbek government support programs for MSMEs, including agricultural borrowers, at a reduced rate of 6%–12% per annum.

The average amount of a microloan is T4.7 million. Real estate is used as underlying collateral, movable and acquired property are used as additional collateral. The delay is 0.86%.

The total amount raised by MFOs with the participation of the NCE amounted to T2.25 billion, of which T2.05 billion is under the Yenbek program through the ACC.

Table A4.19: Performance Indicators of Microfinance Organizations Operating with National Chamber of Entrepreneurs of the Republic of Kazakhstan "Atameken" Participation
(T million)

Region	Authorized capital	Equity capital	Attracted funds				Loans outstanding	NPLs
			2017	2018	2019	Total		
MFO Atameken Mangistau	588	588	160	422.3	300.0	882.3	1,230.1	1.65%
MFO Atameken-Taraz	588	588	235	75.0	260.0	570.0	915.7	–
MFO Kostanay	588	588	259	250.0	89.0	598.0	914.5	0.70%
MFO Atameken Qaragandy	150	45	–	–	200.0	200.0*	61	–
MFO Atameken-Pavlodar	150	15.3	–	–	–	–	28	–
Total	2,064	1,824.3	654	747.3	849.0	2,250.3	3,149.3	0.86%

MFO = microfinance organization, NPL = nonperforming loan

Note: According to the agreement, KazZinc LLP provided a loan (line of credit) to finance entrepreneurs in Karazhal town and Zhairem village worth T200 million for 7 years at 0.1% per annum.

Source: National Chamber of Entrepreneurs of the Republic of Kazakhstan "Atameken."

Table A4.20: Microloans Disbursement
(T million)

Region	2016-2017		2018		2019		Total	
	Σ	number	Σ	number	Σ	number	Σ	number
Mangistau	951.4	156	656.8	143	599.0	106	2,207.2	405
Zhambyl	463.5	113	280.3	89	579.9	117	1,323.7	319
Kostanay	741.7	174	572.7	138	487.7	100	1,802.1	412
Karaganda	-	-	-	-	61.0	7	61.0	7
Pavlodar	-	-	-	-	27.9	5	27.9	5
Total	**2,156.6**	**443**	**1,509.8**	**370**	**1,755.5**	**335**	**5,421.9**	**1,148**

Source: National Chamber of Entrepreneurs of the Republic of Kazakhstan "Atameken."

The NCE notes the benefits of financing carried out through the established MFOs:

- Access to underwriting instruments
- Single-window principle for projects financing
- Mass entrepreneurship development (personal subsidiary economy)
- Involvement of the unemployed and self-employed in the economic turnover
- Yenbek program effectiveness
- Assignment of three elements to one operator (training, financing, support)
- Continuous analysis of the effectiveness of financial support measures for startup projects, flexible modification of loan products
- Full-time and remote technical support through an IT platform that brings together specialists in various fields (agricultural technology, veterinary medicine, public procurement)

Under the current microcredit scheme, the MFOs created by the NCE actively finance start-up projects and use guarantee instruments across four regions, with the level of overdue debts for issued microloans not exceeding 2%, indicating good management by the MFO.

Futher Readings

Alliance for Financial Inclusion.2017. *Bridging the Gender Gap: Promoting Women's Financial Inclusion. Tools and Guidance from the AFI Network.*

Convergences. 2019. *Microfinance Barometer 2019, 10th ed.*, published as part of the 12th Convergences World Forum.

European Commission. 2007. *The Regulation of Microcredit in Europe.*

European Investment Fund. 2019. *European Small Business Finance Outlook.* Working Paper 2019/57.

European Microfinance Network. 2020. *Microcredit Regulation in Europe: An Overview.*

European Microfinance Network and Microfinance Centre. *Microfinance in Europe: Survey Report 2016–2017.*

European Microfinance Platform. 2018. *The Financial Inclusion Compass 2018.*

Global Partnership for Financial Inclusion. *G20 Financial Inclusion Indicators.*

International Finance Corporation. 2017. *MSME Finance Gap.* Washington, D.C.

International Fund for Agricultural Development. 2019. *Creating Opportunities for Rural Youth: 2019 Rural Development Report.*

Microfinance Partnership among MFIs, Banks, Guarantee Funds and National States. 2019. EMN Working Paper N°5.

MIX Market. *Global Outreach & Financial Performance Benchmark Report - 2017-2018.*

National Bank of Kazakhstan. 2020. *Financial Stability Report 2018–1H 2019.*

responsAbility. 2016. *Microfinance Market Outlook: Developments, Forecasts, Trends.*

The World Bank Group. 2017. *Kazakhstan Country Opinion Survey Report.*

The World Bank Group. 2017. *Global Financial Inclusion and Consumer Protection Survey 2017 Report.*

The World Bank Group. 2020. Kazakhstan 2019 Country Profile. *Enterprise Surveys: What Businesses Experience.*

World Bank. 2018. *The Global Findex Database 2017: Measuring Financial Inclusion and the Fintech Revolution.*

www.ingramcontent.com/pod-product-compliance
Lightning Source LLC
Chambersburg PA
CBHW050047220326
41599CB00045B/7318